PUBLIC AND PRIVATE ROLES IN HEALTH CARE SYSTEMS

STATE OF HEALTH SERIES

Edited by Chris Ham, Director of Health Services Management Centre, University of Birmingham

PUBLIC AND PRIVATE ROLES IN HEALTH CARE SYSTEMS

Reform Experience in Seven OECD Countries

Claudia Scott

Open University Press
Buckingham · Philadelphia

Open University Press
Celtic Court
22 Ballmoor
Buckingham
MK18 1XW

e-mail: enquiries@openup.co.uk
world wide web: www.openup.co.uk

and
325 Chestnut Street
Philadelphia, PA 19106, USA

First Published 2001

A catalogue record of this book is available from the British Library

ISBN   0 335 20459 7 (pb)   0 335 20460 0 (hb)

Library of Congress Cataloging-in-Publication Data is available

Typeset by Type Study, Scarborough
Printed in Great Britain by St Edmundsbury Press, Bury St Edmunds,
Suffolk

CONTENTS

SERIES EDITOR'S INTRODUCTION

Health services in many developed countries have come under critical scrutiny in recent years. In part this is because of increasing expenditure, much of it funded from public sources, and the pressure this has put on governments seeking to control public spending. Also important has been the perception that resources allocated to health services are not always deployed in an optimal fashion. Thus at a time when the scope for increasing expenditure is extremely limited, there is a need to search for ways of using existing budgets more efficiently. A further concern has been the desire to ensure access to health care of various groups on an equitable basis. In some countries this has been linked to a wish to enhance patient choice and to make service providers more responsive to patients as 'consumers'.

Underlying these specific concerns are a number of more fundamental developments which have a significant bearing on the performance of health services. Three are worth highlighting. First, there are demographic changes, including the ageing population and the decline in the proportion of the population of working age. These changes will both increase the demand for health care and at the same time limit the ability of health services to respond to this demand.

Second, advances in medical science will also give rise to new demands within the health services. These advances cover a range of possibilities, including innovations in surgery, drug therapy, screening and diagnosis. The pace of innovation quickened as the end of the century approached, with significant implications for the funding and provision of services.

Third, public expectations of health services are rising as those who use services demand higher standards of care. In part, this is stimulated by developments within the health service, including the availability of new technology. More fundamentally, it stems from the emergence of a more educated and informed population, in which people are accustomed to being treated as consumers rather than patients.

Against this background, policy-makers in a number of countries are reviewing the future of health services. Those countries which have traditionally relied on a market in health care are making greater use of regulation and planning. Equally, those countries which have traditionally relied on regulation and planning are moving towards a more competitive approach. In no country is there complete satisfaction with existing methods of financing and delivery, and everywhere there is a search for new policy instruments.

The aim of this series is to contribute to debate about the future of health services through an analysis of major issues in health policy. These issues have been chosen because they are both of current interest and of enduring importance. The series is intended to be accessible to students and informed lay readers as well as to specialists working in this field. The aim is to go beyond a textbook approach to health policy analysis and to encourage authors to move debate about their issue forward. In this sense, each book presents a summary of current research and thinking, and an exploration of future policy directions.

Professor Chris Ham
Director of Health Services Management Centre
University of Birmingham

ACKNOWLEDGEMENTS

This book draws on research which has received financial support from two New Zealand organizations: the Health Research Council and the Faculty of Commerce and Administration, Victoria University of Wellington. My interest in public and private roles and interfaces and in health system reform spans a period of several years, and at various stages valuable research support was provided by Deborah Peikes, Pauline Ng, Kathy Nelson, Evan Roberts and Robbie Lane. In addition, I wish to acknowledge the contributions of a number of New Zealand and overseas colleagues who have provided information, analysis and peer review. Their valuable insights are reflected in the discourse contained within these pages. Any errors or omissions, however, remain, as always the responsibility of the author.

1

INTRODUCTION

The book develops a framework for examining the health reform experiences of seven OECD (Organization for Economic Cooperation and Development) countries with emphasis on the roles of funding, purchasing and provision and the impact of organizational changes on system performance. The seven countries analysed are: Australia, Canada, Germany, the Netherlands, New Zealand, the UK and the United States. All are western democratic societies and some have close affinities arising from former colonial ties or a common language and culture.

The countries vary in size, geographical spread and the levels of private and public sector involvement in the funding, purchasing and provision of health care. With such a wide brief, the coverage of country experiences has been selective rather than comprehensive. Sometimes focus is placed on interesting design features, even when the proposals were not implemented and do not depict the most recent developments.

Over recent years, many governments have introduced changes to the roles of and interfaces between public and private organizations within the health care system. The reforms have modified arrangements for the funding, purchasing and provision of health care. Sometimes reform designs have evolved from considerations within the sector; at other times they have been shaped by economic and public management reforms. Health reforms have placed renewed emphasis on formal contracting arrangements among funders, purchasers and providers. Pressures for greater diversity and responsiveness in services have led to a reduced role for governments in purchasing and providing services, greater decentralization of decision-making, and the delivery of services on a more **competitive** and **contestable** basis.

In some countries this has led to a more strategic role for public sector organizations, centred on the function of governance rather than service delivery. Some countries have adopted a 'big bang' approach to health reform while others have proceeded at a more incremental and leisurely pace. Many reform proposals have suffered 'policy drift', resulting in modification to reform designs during the implementation stage. Trends, influences and policy choices are discussed, including the potential for cross-national learning to inform public policy decision-making in a specific country context.

Some countries with quite diverse system features are now adopting similar strategies for reform. Other countries started from a similar point, but now take divergent pathways. These trends serve to increase the potential for cross-national learning. While each country's reform design reflects a unique inheritance and economic, social and political context, the similarities across reform proposals are striking. One explanation for this is that the forces of globalization and mass communication have increased opportunities for countries to learn from one another. The reforms are important because of the value attached by individuals and groups to health and health care, the influence of health on the achievement of wider societal objectives and the significance of health care's claim on public and private sector resources. Health systems have become more complex, involving diverse approaches to public and private roles and interfaces. In several countries private organizations have attained prominence within health care systems. Countries which have maintained a strong public role have implemented changes that utilize market and market-type instruments and strategies.

The analysis of health care systems can be informed by a number of different disciplinary perspectives. Political scientists provide insights into the distribution of power and the role of stakeholders and interest groups; economists focus on issues surrounding affordability, incentives and problems of **market failure** and **government failure**; sociologists consider the impact of different systems on communities and on particular socio-economic groups. Each discipline contributes its own concepts, theories and frameworks to a rich policy debate.

Some analysts study health reform experiences in the expectation of discovering 'international best practice'. Others do so in search of new ideas and directions, or justification for particular local solutions. Countries can learn from one another, though health system designs need to be fashioned to suit particular circumstances, having regard to values, priorities and the specific country context.

Powerful economic arguments, widely accepted within OECD circles, have linked the poor economic performance of many western countries to high levels of public spending and taxation. From this vantage point, effective health and social policy reforms are central to successful economic strategies for the future. Policymakers are increasingly aware of the linkages between health policy reform and social and economic policy agendas. Interest in reform is widespread in the light of the substantial share of resources devoted to **health care** in many countries. Figure 1.1 shows levels of expenditure on health care as a percentage of gross domestic product (GDP) in the seven chosen countries from 1975 through to the mid-1990s. Comparisons show greater variations in shares among countries in 1998 than in 1975.

Several OECD countries have extended opportunities for private sector organizations to play a larger role in health care systems. While health reforms may be described, somewhat emotively, as involving policy choices between government and markets, most health systems combine government and market elements. Such complex systems involve both public and private organizations, including elements of cooperation and competition, planning and areas where markets operate with a minimum of government interference.

Even in areas where private markets operate freely, most require an underpinning of government to secure property rights, to foster competition, and to guarantee consumer protection. It is common for both public and private organizations to assume a variety of roles, including funding, purchasing, provision, regulation and ownership.

Some public health care organizations are being required to compete with private firms, and greater reliance is being placed on the private sector to support public policy goals. In some countries, increased competition and contestability among public and private sector organizations has been associated with higher transaction costs, raising questions as to whether these changes are justified in terms of gains to efficiency.

The complexity of new health care arrangements means that it is increasingly difficult to classify particular services unequivocally as either public or private (Burchardt 1997). Despite the growing importance of private sector developments within health care

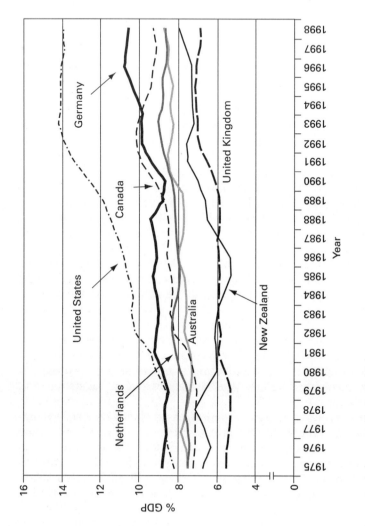

Figure 1.1 Health expenditure as a percentage of GDP, 1975–98
Source: OECD (1998)

systems, public policy advisers in some countries have given insufficient attention to the interactions and interfaces among public and private organizations.

Changes have been made both to the roles assumed by public and private organizations and to the degree to which those roles are separated or combined. Some reforms have brought about greater separation (for example, creating distinct organizations to perform funding and purchasing roles), while others, such as GP fundholding and managed care, have strengthened the linkages across roles.

Public and private interfaces, whether within or across different roles, are becoming more important and more complex. Some countries, while maintaining a strong commitment to public sector financing, are reducing the sector's role in purchasing and provision. New arrangements have shifted responsibilities to health care professionals, individuals and private organizations who act as agents for users and consumers. Issues are being raised concerning the contracting arrangements and accountability provisions for private health professionals who deliver services across both the public and private health care systems.

While there is a trend in several countries for governments to reduce their roles, there are areas such as regulation where government influence over private sector activity is increasing. The more competitive environment surrounding purchasing and service delivery has led to changes involving not only deregulation but also re-regulation, with major impacts on health professionals, purchasers, providers and health care organizations.

Fiscal constraints have led some governments to consider health reform among strategies to limit, or reduce, the coverage provided by the public sector. The introduction of funding systems based on **capitation** and budget caps has helped governments to keep expenditures under control. Some systems have introduced **co-payments**, **co-insurance**, or other provisions that require individuals to meet part of the cost of care. With the notable exception of the United States, many OECD governments assume responsibility for ensuring that citizens have universal access to a basic package of core services. Key issues in health care reform surround the definition of public entitlements and the degree to which public support should target specific groups or provide a uniform entitlement to all citizens.

Policy choices involving the interfaces between public and private organizations are also important in providing for individuals to supplement core services by the purchasing of insurance. Clear public entitlements help individuals to judge their need for supplementary **private insurance** cover. Offsetting the benefits of greater clarity to the user, however, is the increased fiscal risk to the government entailed in making entitlements more explicit.

HEALTH OUTCOMES

Health care services are valued for their positive effects on health outcomes. Better outcomes occur when health status is improved or when care helps to maintain or prevent further deterioration in health status. Health care can be divided into personal health care for individuals and prevention, promotion and protection services for entire populations. Governments have always had a prominent role in overcoming public health risks and this is a major area of concern in less developed countries.

Table 1.1 provides information for the seven selected countries on health status, measured by potential years of life lost due to premature death and by life expectancy at birth. Relating this to Figure 1.1, there does not appear to be a simple positive relationship between health status and the share of resources devoted to health care. In particular, the United States does not perform well, relative to others, in terms of health status measures.

While, traditionally, mortality and morbidity statistics have been

Table 1.1   Health status and outcomes, 1996

Country	Potential years of life lost per 100,000 life years, 1995		Life expectancy at birth (years)	
	Female	Male	Female	Male
Australia	3103	5193	81.1	75.2
Canada	3284	5451	81.5	75.4
Germany	3337	6505	79.9	73.6
Netherlands	3262	5139	80.4	74.7
New Zealand	4775	7342	79.8	74.3
UK	3616	5690	79.3	74.4
United States	4591	8401	79.4	72.7
Average	3709	6246	80.2	74.3

Source: OECD (1998)

relied upon as measures of health status, there is growing agreement that quality of life as well as length of life is important when establishing health status. Defining and measuring health and health outcomes are themselves the subject of policy debate. A medical model of health focuses on the treatment of disease and illnesses, while more holistic approaches to well-being include socio-economic as well as physical aspects of health, and relate individuals to the communities and societies in which they live.

The outcomes of population-based health promotion and disease prevention programmes are often difficult to measure, since the benefits are neither discernible immediately nor easily attributable to specific individuals. Linking improvements in health status to health care is also made difficult by the many factors and influences, other than health care, which affect health status. These factors include adequate housing, income, exercise, food, the company and care of others, a good genetic inheritance and access to a safe and healthy environment.

Perceptions about the determinants of personal and public health will influence views about the appropriate role for the government. Increasingly, personal health is being viewed in the broad context of a community and society, rather than as a characteristic largely attributable to an individual. Measures of health status attach diverse weightings to individual, family, associates and peers, the wider community, the trained health practitioner and society.

Relative, rather than absolute, health status may be the more important influence on an individual's perception of health and their propensity to seek health care. Sometimes the utilization of health services is used to measure health, but this is a poor proxy because it is often influenced by factors such as availability and cost. Health services may also confer other benefits including information and peace of mind. Definitive statements about the domain and range of health outcomes remain elusive and, as in many aspects of health policy, the contributions of different disciplines, which underpin biological, social and economic perspectives, all contribute (Macbeth 1996). Figure 1.2, adapted from an approach used by Hall *et al.* (1993), utilizes the economist's notion of a production function to describe the complex arrangements among inputs, processes, outputs and outcomes in health care. The production analogy clearly shows that both health care and non-health-care inputs and activities contribute to health outputs and outcomes, and that health services influence outcomes other than health. These interrelationships

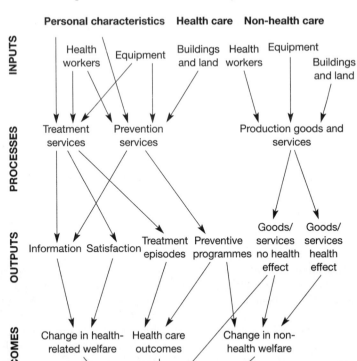

Figure 1.2   Production relationships and health outcomes
Source: Cumming and Scott (1998), adapted from Hall *et al.* (1993)

make it difficult to measure the precise contribution of health care outputs and interventions to maintaining or improving health outcomes.

Policy-makers are placing greater emphasis on measuring the outcomes of health and other interventions, and have become more aware of the influence of lifestyle factors and other socio-economic determinants on health status. Viewing health care in the wider context of economic and social policies requires that alternative approaches to fostering health gains be considered, including measures which reduce tax levels and increase private spending potential. This shift in focus is placing pressure on each **funder**,

purchaser and **provider** of health care to make connections between the production and consumption of health care outputs and improvements in health outcomes.

HEALTH POLICY GOALS

Many countries share policy goals and objectives regarding improvements in the health status and the well-being of their populations. However reform strategies are developed in a country-specific context and may reflect differences in the interpretation of similar goals and in the priorities and trade-offs attached to specific goals. The trend towards a greater sharing of roles with the private sector requires governments view public policy choices within the wider health care system.

The case for shifting the roles and interfaces among public and private organizations must rest on the capacity of different systems to support particular health policy goals. Though many different policy goals influence health system reforms, the discussion here emphasizes efficiency, cost containment, **equity** and choice when looking at system impacts.

Efficiency

Efficiency is concerned with ensuring that resource decisions give value for money, and it is important to distinguish between **allocative** and **technical efficiency**. Allocative efficiency is achieved when the right level and mix of goods and services is produced in the economy. This occurs when the marginal benefit equals the marginal cost, i.e. when the last pound spent on providing a service brings one pound's worth of benefit. Technical efficiency (sometimes termed production efficiency) is achieved when health care outputs (in the form of goods and services) of a given quality are produced at least cost.

Health reforms are often undertaken with a view to improving allocative efficiency by modifying the level and mix of resources devoted to health care. Government strategies for determining the right level are varied, and none are particularly scientific. One approach assumes that existing levels have some legitimacy and so can act as a norm, to which adjustments are made in response to population, technology or policy changes. A second approach measures and benchmarks resource utilization in relation to some

OECD norm. A third approach links appropriateness to macro-economic affordability, as measured by levels of health spending as a percentage of GDP or GNP (gross national product). Although governments are tempted from time to time to justify the level of resources devoted to health care by making comparisons with other countries, the 'correct' level of spending should reflect the values held in a specific country and the degree to which individuals and communities consider that additional health care expenditure will provide benefits which justify the costs.

Concepts of health care efficiency relate both to health care out-puts and to health outcomes. While it is customary to regard the output of health care as particular interventions or services, the efficiency of the outputs of care should ideally be determined by health outcomes, in the form of improvements (or the prevention of deterioration) in health status. The impact of a specific inter-vention will vary across individuals, groups and societies. There-fore, comparisons of efficiency between public and private organizations must allow for variations in the health status of those receiving care.

Cost containment

Concern about levels of economic performance has encouraged a focus on cost containment as a specific health policy goal. While it is possible for cost-containment strategies to both lower costs and improve allocative and technical efficiency, there is no guarantee that this will occur. Cost-containment strategies may lead to efficiency gains, or alternatively, to a shifting of costs, with associated increases in overall system costs. **Cost-shifting** may take place with respect to health care providers, consumers, insurers or others. Public sector cost-containment strategies include measures which shift costs across different public agencies as well as those that limit costs overall.

The effectiveness of cost-containment strategies will depend on the degree to which the government has control over funding and delivery systems. Where facilities are owned publicly and health professionals are salaried, it will be easier for governments to con-tain spending than when health care is delivered privately and no explicit contracts exist between funders, purchasers and providers.

Governments may set budgets in advance for particular cat-egories of health care expenditure, including constraints and ex-penditure limits which apply to both private and public health care professionals and organizations. Public sector cost-containment strategies can also be achieved through measures that influence both the demand for and the supply of services. Strategies to reduce public sector demand include strengthening incentives (including tax concessions) to encourage private spending; measures to encourage or facilitate individuals' opting out of the statutory system; and reductions to the scope and coverage of services. Governments may reappraise the benefits of services with a view to reducing service levels, increasing waiting times, or extending the level of cost-sharing with patients and providers.

Governments can affect supply by controlling the number of medical students and physicians, and the conditions under which providers can obtain reimbursement and funding for services. Public policies may have the ability to alter the number of doctors and hospital beds, the access of individuals to particular procedures and pharmaceuticals, the introduction of new technology, and the locus and nature of the service provided.

As health care systems have become more complex, opportunities to shift the costs of care among various parties have increased. Cost-shifting and cost-containment strategies are often presented as policy measures that will improve efficiency, though sometimes they lead to efficiency losses to the health system as a whole. Public policies need to consider reform strategies in relation to their impacts on both public sector resources and total health system efficiency. Risk management and risk-sharing strategies determine how financial responsibility for the costs of care are to be shared by users, providers, purchasers and funders.

Equity

The goal of equity, when applied to health care systems, concerns what is deemed to be fair in terms of arrangements for the funding, purchasing and delivery of health care. While many would define equity in health care as a basic minimum of care regardless of ability to pay, concepts of fairness are closely interwoven with a society's view of the role of government in the economy and society. In countries where governments play a major role in health care, equity is defined as equal access for equal need, or even equal outcomes, the latter requiring a targeting of resources to those with the poorest health status. In other countries, however, access to health care is linked to employment and income status, and this too, is regarded as fair.

Equity can be defined in relation to geographical area, age, cultural and social background and kind of disability or illness. The term 'equity' can refer to the spread and ease of access to services as well as the appropriateness of the services to particular groups. There is often tension between the rights of individuals to exercise freedom of choice in behaviour and lifestyle, and the right of society to use coercive powers to encourage and constrain the consumption of health care. Equity in health refers to redistribution from the well to the ill, not merely a redistribution from rich to poor. Designing regimes for targeting assistance for health care is more complex than for services like education and housing, since resource requirements must be related both to health risk and to affordability.

Countries vary in the degree to which they aim to promote equity in the distribution of health status and health care. A society's view of fairness depends on the degree to which health care is perceived as different from other goods or services. When health care is regarded as similar to other goods and services, and access is based on the income and employment status of individuals, governments will be reluctant to constrain individuals from purchasing additional health care with private resources. Some societies subsidize access to health care because they consider it to be a right, similar to rights of citizenship. The term 'positive rights' is used to describe the basic rights of citizens to health care and other social services, and to distinguish them from negative rights, such as freedom from interference. If health is treated as a positive right, this gives governments a mandate to treat access to health care differently from access to other goods and services.

Equity rarely means equality in the sense of all individuals receiving an identical or equivalent level of health care or enjoying the same health status. There will always be inequalities in health status and access to health care. Even setting aside the influences of genetic inheritance, education, income and lifestyles, individuals will have different preferences regarding acceptable levels of risk and desirable levels of care. Interventions by society in health care serve to moderate inequalities to a point where the differences among citizens are regarded as acceptable.

Considering health care as a production function, the meaning of equity or fairness can be related to inputs, processes, outputs or outcomes. One concept of equity places emphasis on equal access to inputs, processes and outputs for equal need. Another aims to achieve equal outcomes rather than equal inputs or processes. The particular interpretation will influence both the nature and scale of the intervention and also the degree to which it targets resources, with a view to reducing differences in health status across the population.

Choice

The policy goal of choice pertains to issues surrounding access to health care and health care insurance. Few health care systems give autonomous individuals choice of service. Insurance is usually involved, and even in private systems, insurers and employers are influential in determining the level and nature of services received. When health care systems are funded by the public, the effective purchaser of the service is the government rather than the individual.

Choice in health care is increased with the range of health care interventions, technologies and providers, purchasers and insurers that individuals can access. Linked to the policy goal of choice is the notion of voice. Voice is increased when individuals and communities participate and have representation in health system decision-making. In health care markets, the preferences and interests of users of the service are often subservient to the preference of the funder, purchaser or provider of care.

The level of choice which is given to individuals or groups within a health care system is often related to the entitlement to care as defined by either a public or private funder. When substantial public funding is involved, governments have considerable potential to exert influence over the price, quantity and quality of health care that is delivered.

The health policy literature identifies several other health policy goals, including **accountability** and quality. Various elements of accountability can be identified, including political accountability, professional accountability and managerial accountability. The growing complexity of health care arrangements has increased the accountability requirements on public and private organizations and has led to greater attention being given to performance evaluation and monitoring.

Quality of care has also become an important policy goal, though perceptions of quality will vary among patients, politicians, managers, clinicians and other actors within the health care system. Not unlike the production of health care, quality can be related to inputs, processes, outputs or outcomes. Increasingly, quality is

perceived as something which transcends organizational boundaries and is system-wide. Quality occurs when good decisions
regarding care are made so that resources are utilized effectively
and better health outcomes are produced.

Designing a health care system which ranks highly across several
policy goals is a difficult task. Particular goals are interpreted vari-
ously, as are the concepts of health and health outcomes. Although
health reforms sometime achieve gains across a number of different
policy goals, it is also common for gains in one area to be made at the
expense of another. Over time, systems may alter the priority
attached to particular goals, as some system design features prove
more effective than others in achieving specific goals and objectives.
The complexity of health care systems means that inevitably, and
particularly within public health systems, there are diverse expectations among stakeholder groups, including the public, those receiving health care, politicians, managers and public sector agencies.

PLAN OF THE BOOK

This book adopts a comparative policy approach in discussing the
systems and approach to health system reform experiences in seven
OECD countries. Comparative public policy analysis is defined
more appropriately as an approach and method rather than a distinct area of public policy studies. Comparative public policy
evolved during the 1960s and 1970s, but was limited by inadequate
attention to the context within which public policies were developed and by unrealistic expectations of the potential for studies in
one country to provide policy lessons for others. De Leon and
Resnick-Terry (1998) suggest that conditions exist for a renaissance
in comparative policy analysis arising from a growing number of
transnational policy issues, advances in communication technology
and new conceptual bases.

A large policy literature reports varying degrees of optimism and
pessimism concerning the benefits and pitfalls of making comparisons across countries to inform policy choices within a country.
Rudolph Klein compares cross-national learning to 'a multi-ring
circus with different actors performing in each of them' (Klein 1995:
7). Alan Maynard observes that the reluctance of physicians to be
confused by facts in their everyday practice is paralleled by the
reluctance of policy-makers to be informed by evidence when
'redisorganizing' health care systems in pursuit of perfection in

equity, efficiency and cost control (Maynard 1995: 49). Marmor suggests that comparative policy analysis suffers not only from the World Cup fallacy but also from the fallacy of comparative difference: the first aims to locate the best approach and to apply it indiscriminately to all other countries; the second suggests that the unique context surrounding any country limits the potential for learning across countries (Marmor, in Altenstetter and Bjorkman 1997).

Various approaches can be taken to applying the comparative method. A common approach has been to draw on the expertise of different country experts and to compile information from which to make comparisons. Some authors have used international databases and statistical techniques to explain variations across countries and to draw correlations across different variables (Heidenheimer *et al.* 1990; Castles 1999). Utilizing data and input from various sources inevitably compromises the comparability of those data and can qualify the conclusions drawn from such studies (OECD 1992, 1994; Ham 1997; Raffel 1997; Ranade 1998). The approach taken in this book is to develop an analytical framework which can be applied uniformly across the countries, clarifying the similarities and differences and thus facilitating cross-country comparisons. A second point of difference is the explicit attention which is given to the roles and interfaces of public and private organizations within health care systems.

Chapter 2 discusses roles and interfaces within health care systems, building on the discussion of health policy goals in this chapter. The separate roles of funding, purchasing, provision, regulation and ownership are defined, and consideration is given to interfaces within and between roles. Specific attention is given to three reform strategies which have been adopted in several OECD countries: the **purchaser–provider split**, **managed competition** and **managed care**. Theories of market failure and government failure are outlined briefly and provide frameworks within which to consider the merits of government intervention in the markets for health insurance and health care.

Health systems in Germany and the Netherlands are treated in Chapter 3, the US, Canadian and Australian systems in Chapter 4 and the UK and New Zealand systems in Chapter 5. Coverage of each country is selective, and discussion is focused on public and private roles and interfaces, reform proposals and aspects of system performance in relation to the policy goals of efficiency, cost containment, equity and choice. Chapter 6 draws on earlier chapters and other literature to reflect on trends and issues in health system reform. Further consideration is given to the potential benefits of cross-national learning and to key public policy choices surrounding public and private roles and interfaces.

2

PUBLIC AND PRIVATE ROLES IN HEALTH CARE

Public and private organizations undertake a number of roles within health care systems, including funding, purchasing, provision, regulation and ownership. Arrangements surrounding these roles and interfaces affect system performance in relation to health outcomes and specific policy goals. This chapter starts by considering the roles and interfaces of public and private organizations in health care. It then looks at some approaches to classify health care systems before going on to describe three popular reform strategies: the purchaser–provider split, managed competition and managed care. The theory of market (and government) failure is discussed and linked to policy debates about the appropriate role for public and private organizations within health care systems.

It is useful to define the various roles which can be undertaken within a health care system; however, precise definitions are difficult in that roles are defined differently in the context of different health care systems. Public and private interfaces in health care systems refer to the boundaries between and linkages among public and private organizations within a health care system. Roles and interfaces among public and private organizations may be simple or complex. Sometimes a public or private organization performs a single role; alternatively, it may undertake several. For example, in the UK, GP fundholding practices not only provide primary care services but also purchase selected hospital services on behalf of patients. In some health care systems, public and private organizations have roles in common, whereas in others, roles are assigned primarily or exclusively to public or private organizations.

Interfaces, like roles, are sometimes clear but more often are not. In Canada, interfaces between private and public insurance are clearly defined and private insurers are prohibited from insuring services in private hospitals which are deemed 'necessary' and covered through public insurance. Sometimes, public and private organizations compete with one another, but more commonly the roles are complementary. For example, in the UK and Australia, private insurance covers the cost of a room and treatment carried out by a private consultant in a public hospital.

Health reforms have challenged the traditional assignment of roles and interfaces among public and private organizations, raising policy questions such as:

* Which roles (if any) should a government perform alone and which should be shared with private sector organizations, and on what basis?
* What assignment of public and private roles and interfaces is likely to be effective in improving health outcomes and system performance in relation to particular health policy goals?

Health system reforms have given emphasis to the role of private organizations in the achievement of public policy goals and objectives, to the use of market and quasi-market approaches to health care and to greater competition and contestability among public and private organizations. Reform designs have been influenced by economic ideas and concepts and by the 'new public management' literature which has shaped public sector and governance changes in several OECD countries. Elements of these reforms including clarifying the roles of government, improved systems of performance management, and greater transparency and accountability surrounding government activities.

Systems vary in the degree to which access is influenced by public and private funders, purchasers, providers or consumers. Sometimes there is a tidy relationship between a particular role and a specific organization responsible for the activity. More often, public and private organizations may each carry out more than one role, and one role may be carried out by more than one organization. In the 1990s, for example, the role of purchasing was carried out by both health authorities and GP fundholders in the UK.

THE FUNDING ROLE

A public and private funder is an organization which finances care on behalf of individuals, employers, the government or other groups. Funding roles may be undertaken by employers, public or private insurers, central (federal) or local government units, unions, charitable or friendly societies and others. Funders may derive revenue from a range of sources, including taxes, insurance premiums and out-of-pocket payments.

Both public and private funding may be involved in meeting the cost of a particular service, and interfaces between these funding arrangements will vary. For example, in New Zealand, a private insurance policy may reimburse the cost of a government-imposed part-charge on patients, and even provide a daily cash payment for days spent in a public hospital. The nature of these interfaces affects how costs are shared among public and private funders.

Costs of health care will vary among individuals depending on their age, genetic inheritance and socio-economic position. Health care expenditures exhibit much greater variation from year to year for households than do other goods and services. Individuals may seek insurance to protect themselves against the small probability of a large loss. **Risk-pooling** within a group makes it possible to predict future losses for that group in a way that is not possible for individuals. Private insurers provide peace of mind to their customers and make payments (or provide services) to those individuals who are unfortunate enough to experience the insured risk.

Private insurers are reluctant to insure those for whom there is certainty of a loss, since there is no risk to assume. To the individual contemplating joining an insurance pool, the perceived ideal is a pay-out from the insurer, upon loss, which equals the actuarial mean of the probabilities in the risk pool. However, a private insurance company requires that pay-outs are less than premiums, to allow for administration and some profit or return to shareholders.

Experience rating is a practice used by commercial insurance companies to relate premiums to estimates of the likely health care costs of individuals or groups. Experience rating allows insurers to offer discounts to clients with lower risk and also to those who agree to limit their risk, for example by embracing healthy lifestyles. **Community rating** ignores these differences to varying degrees and pricing offers limited scope to reflect particular individual or group risks.

In the European context, **social insurance** relates to sickness funds which finance health care by contributions from employers and employees. A social insurance system detaches contributions from expected risk levels and redistributes wealth from individuals with low expectations of loss to those with higher risk levels. Tax-financed systems allow redistribution to be related both to risk and to income. Even when the public contributions carry the title 'premium', they are commonly community-rated and are not linked to the risk status of a particular individual. Social insurance shares with private insurance the characteristics of risk-pooling and risk transfer, but also has important redistributive elements that are not found in private insurance.

In the context of proposed health reforms in the Netherlands and New Zealand, the term social insurance assumes a different meaning again. Social insurance referred to a public scheme in which individual tax contributions were pooled and financed health vouchers whose value was set having regard to levels of health risk and ability to pay. The vouchers allowed individuals to purchase an insurance policy covering basic health care from a number of competing public and private insurers or purchasers.

In the US context, the phrase 'national health insurance' is used to describe programmes which make comprehensive health care universally accessible at a certain standard of quality and within certain cost limits. Sometimes the term 'insurance' is used loosely to refer to specific programmes such as **Medicare** and **Medicaid**, and programmes where government revenues are used to guarantee universal access to basic health care.

While the demand for health insurance cover will reflect the health status, income and risk preferences of consumers, the need for health care may arise from unforeseen circumstances, such as accidents and public health risks. Societies may consider individuals to be poorly equipped to make good assessments of these risks, and prefer social insurance, which allows for a greater pooling of risk across individuals. Private insurers have much stronger incentives for pricing in relation to risk than do social insurers, since they use this information to establish the level of premiums (Rejda 1984).

THE PURCHASING ROLE

A purchaser is an individual or organization that makes arrangements for health care to be accessed. Sometimes the purchaser assumes some of the financial risk associated with health care purchasing decisions. In a traditional indemnity plan the insurer takes on a high degree of risk exposure, since all payments to providers must be met by premiums. The risk profile may be moderated by shifting some of the assigned risk to funders, other purchasers, providers or consumers. At other times, the purchaser serves as an administrative conduit between funders and providers. Depending on the nature of the arrangements, purchasers ensure, at a minimum, that bills are paid, but may also take responsibility for organizing the activities of providers. In such cases, the agency merely manages the flow of funds and earns profits in the form of management fees. It has no exposure to risk arising from gaps between premium revenues and payments to providers.

A **monopsonist** is a single large buyer of health care which can exert considerable influence over market prices. When a government funds and contracts for services on behalf of large populations it acts as a monopsonist, influencing both the price paid and what others will pay for the same services. The role of purchasing became an important feature of health reform proposals in the late 1980s and 1990s, and many OECD countries experimented with developing a purchasing function separate from that of funding and provision. The reforms were popular in systems which had integrated systems of purchasing and delivery and were seen as a possible vehicle for improving both allocative and technical efficiency. Even in Germany and the Netherlands, where separate purchasing agencies do not exist, the government is encouraging the sickness funds to become more proactive purchasers, as a strategy to improve the quality and efficiency of the health care system.

THE PROVIDER ROLE

A provider is a health professional or a public or private organization that is involved in the delivery of health care services. Under traditional indemnity insurance arrangements, providers do not share the risk of health expenditures since remuneration is based on fee-for-service. However, many health care arrangements now have remuneration provisions which allow providers to assume some financial risk. Financial risk is highest when a provider agrees to deliver all the care that is needed by a given population for a set fee. It is positive when fees are prospectively set, as with Medicare in the United States, and in systems where payment is subject to penalty or reward depending on measures of the level and efficiency of services provided.

The roles of public and private organizations in health care provision is diverse across systems. In general, private providers, such as GPs, family physicians and various other health care professionals, will be important in the delivery of primary or ambulatory care. Not-for-profit private providers often deliver care to the elderly, hospice and disability services, and sometimes hospital care. Public involvement in delivery is more likely at the secondary care level. The trend in many health care systems is to extend opportunities for both for-profit and not-for-profit providers to offer health care services under contract to the public sector.

THE OWNERSHIP AND REGULATORY ROLES

Regulation

Government regulation is a prominent feature of most health care finance and delivery systems. A government may impose regulations to influence the scope and nature of a health insurance package, to improve access by particular groups and also to increase the potential viability of the insurer. Regulations also affect the nature and delivery of the care available, and the ability of particular kinds of provider and institution to deliver the service and affect arrangements surrounding the ownership and operation of hospitals, pharmacies and other health care facilities.

Sometimes regulatory roles are undertaken by professional organizations and societies acting under a legal framework with respect to registration, certification and disciplinary matters. Various measures aim to restrict access and utilization. Governments can reduce the number of individuals trained in the health professions and levels of subsidies for professional education. Hospital supply may be checked by limiting the growth of capital spending. While many such regulations are imposed by the public sector, the effects apply to private sector organizations, and to the interface between public and private funders, purchasers and providers. Contracting and regulatory arrangements may not affect the particular GP or primary care provider directly, but via some association or professional body. Government contracts, made at arm's length with professional bodies of practitioners, specialists and other health care providers, offer a zone of autonomy and independence for individual health providers.

Regulatory approaches span a wide range, from command-and-control actions and orders on a case by case basis, to more general policies governing finance and service delivery. Regulations are essential to developing competitive markets for health insurance, purchasing and service delivery. Market transactions commonly take place in the context of a set of implicit or explicit rules including, for example, the laws governing property, torts and contracts. Regulations specific to a particular sector like health may be required to supplement administrative institutions and the general legal rules governing transactions. Public providers may be subject to different regulatory and legal requirements from private providers.

Definitions of regulation often reflect particular disciplines, and include economic, legal and public administration perspectives. Mitnick (1980) defines regulation as policing of a private activity with respect to a rule prescribed in the public interest. This view portrays the government as agent, and consumers or interest groups as principal. Others see regulations as the outcome of a process of bargaining and negotiation among consumers, firms and **regulators**.

Three categories of health care regulations can be distinguished: economic, social and subsidiary regulation. Economic regulations cover market aspects of industry behaviour (price, quality and quantity of service, competitive practices); social regulation is directed at unsafe or unhealthy products and harmful by-products of the production process; and subsidiary regulations implement medical and social security benefit programmes.

Health care delivery systems provide examples of regulations in all three of these categories. Controls on prices, quality and quantity of health care services are common, as are restrictions on inputs such as pharmaceuticals, and procedures for the registration and licensing of health care providers and institutions. Health care finance and insurance systems are noted for subsidiary regulation that defines benefits packages, conditions of access and entitlement and interfaces between public entitlements and private finance and insurance arrangements.

Reforms which rely on market and quasi-market mechanisms for the funding and delivery of health care often require more regulation than do systems dominated by public sector funding, provision and delivery. In particular, policy reforms which enhance competition among funders, purchasers and providers may require a more detailed regulatory framework. Regulations are required to guarantee patients' rights, promote quality and provide consumer protection through utilization review, medical audit, performance indicators and other types of public disclosure about services and service providers.

A large area for potential government regulation is the relationships between funders, purchasers and providers. Where a centrally mandated state entitlement exists, there is a need to specify its boundaries and to prescribe opportunities for cost-sharing and the supplementation of services. While the trend is recently to arm's-length transactions rather than vertical integration, purchasers have a major role in guaranteeing the effectiveness and efficiency of funding and delivery systems.

When a government subsidizes access to health care, it is likely to impose regulations on certain aspects of the service, such as those affecting the quantity, quality and price. By controlling price per unit, quantity or quality of service or a combination of these factors, governments can affect their own exposure to risk.

Rising costs of health care reflect the introduction of new technology, and the more intensive treatment of particular population groups, such as neonates and the elderly. Regulation constraining the development and introduction of new technology can be a powerful weapon in the battle against rising health care costs.

Ownership

The ownership role in health care is related to the property rights surrounding the physical and intellectual capital associated with health care finance, purchasing and delivery arrangements. Private insurers may have shareholders with ownership interests, whereas in public systems, the ownership interest often remains with the government. Recent health reforms have encouraged debate over whether it is necessary for governments to maintain their ownership interest in hospitals and other organizations providing health care services. The Private Finance Initiative in the UK provides an example where private investment in public health facilities has been encouraged.

Reforms have led to greater awareness of the potential for conflict between the purchasing and the ownership role. In the 1993 New Zealand reforms, a clearer separation of the government's ownership and purchasing interests was made, and reinforced by creating separate ministerial portfolios.

MARKET FAILURE IN HEALTH CARE

Theories of market failure provide possible rationale for government intervention: to provide public goods and internalize **externalities**; to overcome **cream-skimming** and other inefficiencies in the market for private insurance; to address information problems and improve competition and contestability in providing markets; and to guarantee access to health care for groups who have insufficient resources. In a World Bank report on public and private roles in health, Musgrove (1996: 1) suggests:

> there does not seem to be a sharp peak of ideal public and private relations rising above the plateau. The most important conclusions or recommendations for public policy then have to do with assuring a place on the plateau and avoiding the numerous chasms that surround it. These chasms, which represent failures of various kinds, result from too much, too little, or the wrong kind of state intervention.

To avoid these failures, policy-makers need to have some basis for making informed decisions as to when the government should intervene in the health care system. Some insights on these issues can be gleaned from the theory of market failures, which explains some of the limitations of relying on private markets in the funding and delivery of health care. Although the theory does not prescribe the roles which governments should adopt in health care systems, it offers a useful framework for thinking about policy choices surrounding the roles of public and private organizations within health care systems.

One way to reflect on market failures in health care is to compare them with private markets in which consumers and producers are the key drivers of decisions about what, how and for whom goods and services will be produced and distributed. Economic theory assumes that consumer preferences are somehow intrinsic to individuals and independent of producers, and that consumers have full knowledge of the benefits of different consumption choices.

Markets for the supply of and demand for many types of health care do not behave like markets for other goods and services. In a normal market, consumers and producers are relatively independent of one another. There are many consumers and producers, which means that no buyer or seller is large enough to have a major impact on the market price.

In health care systems, on the other hand, decisions regarding funding and delivery systems are shaped by governments who fund and purchase services on behalf of entire populations. When this occurs, choices made by individual consumers give way to collective decisions made by governments in the public interest.

Table 2.1 identifies various sources of market failure in health care funding and delivery systems.

Public goods

Public goods are defined as activities which are both non-rival and non-excludable. A good is non-rival when the act of consuming it does not reduce quantity, and therefore additional persons can consume it at zero marginal cost. A good is non-excludable if, once provided, it is available to everyone, a feature which will make individuals unwilling to pay money in order to get access. Public goods are defined in theoretical terms and few examples exist of pure public goods. Some activities have similar characteristics, however, such as street-lighting or the defence system: once provided it is difficult to exclude individuals and an additional person may benefit from the service at zero cost. Markets cannot provide public

Table 2.1   Sources of market failure in health care

Source	*Government policy responses*
Public goods	Taking responsibility for public health strategies and care
	Provision of information as basis for health care decision-making
	Support for research and development
Externalities	Funding or subsidization of health insurance and/or provision of health care
Insurance markets	Regulation of insurance markets
	Operation of a residual scheme
Provider markets	Regulation of health providers and organizations
	Consumer protection
	Measures to address monopolies
Income distribution	Funding of care on a universal or selective basis
	Providing income supplementation for high-risk and/or low-income groups

Source: Weimer and Vining (1999)

goods efficiently because individuals will prefer to be 'free-riders' and enjoy the service once it becomes available, rather than paying for it. These difficulties mean that markets will undersupply public goods and goods which resemble them.

Population-based programmes for disease prevention and health promotion services resemble public goods in that consumption is non-rival, and the marginal cost of an additional person is very small or zero. Information and research and development expenditures, which underpin and inform a health care system, may also have public good elements, and therefore inadequate levels of investment and information-sharing may occur if matters are left exclusively to markets and private decision-makers.

Externalities

Market failure may arise because benefits and costs from particular health care interventions extend beyond producers and consumers to third parties: these benefits and costs are known as externalities. If individuals receive benefits from health care delivered to others, this benefit cannot easily be expressed through market forces. Leaving the level of resources devoted to health care exclusively to private markets will result in too little of the service being purchased. Moreover, benefits to third parties can be shared and therefore have attributes and characteristics which resemble those of public goods.

Insurance markets

Insurance allows people to pool resources so that the collective contributions of the group can meet the expenses of those who require care. However, problems may arise which lead to inefficiencies in the market for health insurance. One problem is **moral hazard**, whereby people become careless in respect of those risks for which they are insured. Another is **adverse selection**, whereby those who seek out insurance are more likely than the average person to use it. Concerns about adverse selection mean that insurers exhibit **risk aversion** and are unwilling to offer cover to companies which are small, and whose workers are high risk. Problems lessen as the size of an insurance pool increases, since the law of large numbers guarantees that the average costs of large groups will exhibit a smaller deviation around the mean than will a small group.

Analysis reveals very different levels of health expenditure when populations are stratified by age, ethnic and cultural background. Most health care systems find that a significant part of total expenditure is spent on a relatively small portion of the total population. An estimate based on the US system suggests that, in any one year, 1 per cent of the population consumes 25 per cent of all expenditure, while 5 per cent accounts for more than 50 per cent of all health care outlays (Aaron and Schwartz 1984). In response to adverse selection, insurers seek out low-risk clients who will make minimum calls on the pool. They use screening measures to filter out individuals with high risk profiles, resulting in a situation where such individuals incur difficulty in securing cover.

Adverse selection generates pressures on policy-makers to offset the inability or unwillingness of private markets to offer insurance. Experience rating is an inevitable outgrowth of any competitive insurance market. In competitive private insurance markets, firms providing community rating will eventually be forced to shift to experience rating, to avert falling profits, as low-risk customers depart in search of experience-rated insurance at a lower premium. Efforts to raise premiums overall will simply speed up the outflow of low-risk customers. This process is documented by Blue Cross and Blue Shield in the United States, which operated initially on the basis of community rating, but later shifted to experience rating.

Some international experts argue that the positive incentive and efficiency effects of experience rating are not outweighed by the administrative overheads associated with the system. Others suggest that efficiency gains from experience rating can only be justified when it is possible to control the risk factors: for example, conditions in the workplace and personal behaviour characteristics.

Provider markets

Health care provider markets may result in economies of scale or scope or market failures arising from the existence of monopolies. A **monopolist** holds a dominant position in the market and reduces welfare by restricting output and charging higher prices than would occur if there were competing suppliers. In health care, market failures may result from a serious imbalance of information between users and providers of care. Consumers lack perfect information about the outputs, outcomes and quality of services produced.

Providers have superior information, and incentives may encourage the supply of services beyond the optimal point where marginal cost equals marginal benefit.

Many health care services are consumed infrequently, and consumers may be too sick to make a wise choice at shopping time. The impacts of health interventions are difficult to predict and it is often hard to measure the contribution to health outcomes of health care, apart from a wide range of other socio-economic determinants. Governments may intervene to regulate providers, offer consumer protection, and encourage the development of competitive and contestable markets as strategies for overcoming these problems.

Income distribution

The **inverse care law** suggests that those who are likely to require the most resources for health care will tend to be those who can least afford to pay. The inability of some to afford basic health insurance cover is identified as a possible source of market failure. Even if private markets offer insurance, it may be at a price which is so high that it is unaffordable. Thus market failure may arise because of a poor matching between the level of risk present and the availability of income to purchase insurance.

GOVERNMENT FAILURE

While theories of market failure in health care and health insurance have featured prominently in the health care literature, there is growing recognition that the mere existence of market failure does not provide both a necessary and sufficient condition for governments to intervene. Policy-makers must justify interventions and ensure that benefits outweigh costs. While a society may suffer welfare losses arising from market failure, interventions by governments impose costs, potentially resulting in government failure.

The theory of government failure is not as comprehensive and accepted as that of market failure, though many possible sources have been identified. According to social choice theory, governments may fail because of problems arising from the use of voting rules and other processes surrounding collective choice. Political and bureaucratic processes can result in rent-seeking behaviour, vote-trading, short time horizons and other behaviours which lead to poor-quality decision-making. In particular, politicians may adopt policy positions which give precedence to political rather than economic and social benefits.

Another major set of failures arises from problems in the bureaucratic supply of services. Governments, unlike private firms, do not need to survive in the marketplace. The absence of pressure from consumers can lead to the delivery of services which are inefficient and lack responsiveness. Decentralized governments, while more responsive to citizens, are more complex in administrative terms and can lead to fiscal externalities, resulting from a poor matching of tax burdens and expenditure benefits (Weimer and Vining 1999).

Reforms in several countries have altered the roles and interfaces between public and private roles. System reforms involving internal or 'quasi' markets have subjected public and private organizations to competition. The interplay among individuals and public and private organizations performing various roles within the health care system have altered the nature of risk-sharing arrangements among individuals, employers, health care organizations and governments.

THE PURCHASER–PROVIDER SPLIT, MANAGED COMPETITION AND MANAGED CARE

The purchaser–provider split describes reforms in which the role of purchasing health care has been separated from that of providing services. This feature was an important part of health reform proposals in both the UK and New Zealand, and led to the establishment of public hospitals as stand-alone units, reporting to a board of directors. The separation encouraged public purchasers to make conscious choices as to the services they required, and fostered greater competition and contestability among public and private health providers. The purchaser–provider split opened up new alternatives to traditional modes of service delivery, facilitated the shifting of care from institutional to community settings and reduced the dominance of particular providers and providing organizations. The reform resulted in a much clearer specification of contracts with providers and strengthened the incentives on providers to be more responsive to those receiving care. It also served to improve information on the price, volume and quality of services and established clearer lines of public accountability for purchasing and provider roles.

Managed competition describes a market in which insurers compete with one another to offer health insurance and also health care. Managed competition, sometimes called regulated competition, requires a basic package to be defined, so that insurers can compete and individuals and employers can make informed comparisons across different health care plans. Governments are often involved in defining or influencing the nature of basic benefit coverage, including measures to deter insurers from engaging in risk selection by offering packages which are unattractive to high-risk groups.

In Germany and the Netherlands, the term managed competition describes a system in which there is regulated competition among public and private insurers to deliver a set of core services. In the US context, variants of the managed competition approach include third-party management, the traditional group- or staff-model health maintenance organization (HMO) and the risk-bearing gatekeeper model (Jérôme-Forget *et al.* 1995). The proposed Clinton administration reforms were described as managed competition within a global budget.

Managed care describes a range of strategies which involve close linkages among particular service providers and those who fund or purchase health care. In the US environment, managed care was a response to the traditional indemnity insurance model, whereby doctors were paid fee-for-service and neither the patient nor the provider had incentives to be cost conscious, since premiums were often met by employers. Most managed care schemes involve the provision of a set of comprehensive health services to those enrolled in the scheme for a prepaid premium.

Managed care schemes are associated with ongoing utilization review and quality control and assurance measures. Schemes often have incentives for those enrolled to utilize certain providers and facilities, though some schemes allow greater choice, if the patient is willing to meet a higher co-payment for the service. Some managed care schemes employ doctors directly, while others do not, but require them to assume some financial risk and responsibility for cost control. Within the context of systems which are reliant on public funding, the term 'managed' (or integrated) care is used to refer to strategies which offer a seamless approach to service delivery, incorporating strategies for prevention as well as treatment and facilitating the movement of patients between hospital and community settings.

Weiner and de Lissovoy (1993) offer a comprehensive

classification system for managed care and health insurance plans which draws attention to contractual relationships, both formal and informal, underlying arrangements for medical care delivery and financing. The taxonomy provides for six different kinds of health insurance plan, which are then classified according to the degree to which the financing risk of the plan rests primarily on insurers, intermediaries or physicians. Consumers may also assume risk, through various arrangements involving **deductibles** and co-insurance. The taxonomy identifies the extent to which restrictions are placed on the consumer's selection of provider, the presence or absence of significant utilization controls on the practice of providers and the existence of an obligation by the plan to provide care via a network. The last two elements are useful in distinguishing health care plans which involve managed care, meaning an integrated delivery system which manages the care received by consumers, from managed competition in which many organizations compete with one another to insure and purchase a package of care.

DEFINING PUBLIC ENTITLEMENTS

When both public and private organizations are involved in funding, purchasing and provision, it is important to define the roles and responsibility of each and the conditions under which individuals may receive access to care or become eligible for public or private subsidy. Definitions of entitlement, described as core services (or a basic benefits package), are important in shaping the scope and coverage of private and social insurance schemes.

The literature on concepts of core is extensive, and draws on several disciplines including epidemiology, economics, political philosophy and ethics. It includes discussion of the various concepts and definitions of core which have been adopted in different countries (Ham and Honigsbaum, in Saltman *et al.* 1998, Cumming *et al.* 1994). Approaches to defining public entitlement operate at both the macro and micro levels, and exhibit varying degrees of public participation and explicitness.

Defining core services helps individuals and communities to discover service priorities and preferences, and encourages equitable access to care. Many different approaches to defining public entitlement are observed. Some concepts of core define broad categories of care to be covered, leaving decisions regarding the level and distribution of treatment to health professionals and individuals. Alternatively, a more methodical approach can be adopted, involving criteria and an assessment process to determine eligibility. Another approach defines core services as those which are cost-effective. Health interventions are often person-specific, and measures of cost-effectiveness require judgements about the likely gain which will result if a person receives a particular treatment.

An explicit core provides greater clarity of entitlement than an implicit core, and improves the accountability of funders, purchasers and providers. Knowledge of the publicly defined core allows users to arrange supplementary insurance which provides quicker access or higher quality core services and also services outside the core. If definitions of core services support improved health outcomes and health gain, then greater clarity and transparency of the core will encourage technical and allocative efficiency.

Health reforms in the 1990s have given attention to the development of evidence-based health care. The term is not new and refers to the use of scientific evidence to guide decision-making in the area of policy, health and medical practice. The International Cochrane Collaboration (formed in 1992) established methods for carrying out systematic reviews that synthesize and generate information from research studies which are published on the Internet and on CD-Rom. This has encouraged the development of general and specialist databases and stimulated other processes to facilitate systematic review, such as the NHS Centre for Reviews and Dissemination at York. Systems must be established which disseminate findings to users and create environments in which information and research are valued as inputs to decision-making (Frommer and Rubin, in Bloom 2000).

Research on the effectiveness of interventions, including assessments of new technologies, is part of a wide range of strategies used to measure the cost-effectiveness of health care interventions. The use of formulae, models and quality-adjusted life-years (QALY) league tables provides opportunities for making judgements about investments in health care and their likely contribution to health gain. Programme budgeting including marginal analysis establishes priorities for resources by examining the costs and benefits involved in making marginal shifts to existing resource allocations.

Considerable attention has been given to the work of the Dunning Committee in the Netherlands (Dunning 1992) which established various tests to determine the basic health care package, including: whether the care was necessary from the community's point of view, whether the care was effective and efficient, and whether the care could be left to personal responsibility. In Oregon in the United States, the state decided to establish priorities for individuals covered by the Medicaid programme, which meant that support could be extended to a larger population. The Oregon plan was implemented in 1994 and involves over five hundred condition–treatment pairs. While successful in expanding the population coverage, the methodology has not been adopted for use by all individuals in the state.

Governments are being challenged as they try to define processes for engaging the public in setting limits to public entitlement and priorities for public funding. Processes need to achieve the desired results and also avoid dominance by particular provider and interest groups. In the New Zealand reforms, core services was defined as those services 'to which ... everyone should have access, on affordable terms and without unreasonable waiting time' (Upton 1991). The Core Services Committee, which was asked to define core services, decided to reject any approach that would eliminate whole treatments. Over time its emphasis shifted to the establishment of guidelines to govern priorities within particular services. This led the Committee to work closely with providers in order to identify priority areas within services which can improve health gains.

Even when major investments are made in priority-setting, as has occurred in the Netherlands and New Zealand, there may be a rather tenuous relationship between research findings and the day-to-day operation of a health care system. Problems exist in shifting resources to new purposes in a constrained financial environment. Even when cost-effectiveness can be demonstrated, there is no guarantee that such services will be affordable to a government. Weak links may exist between the findings of this research and the contracting and accountability arrangements of decision-makers regarding funding, purchasing and provision.

Defining core services can be effective in acknowledging the limits to government's willingness to assume risk, but the definition of an explicit core creates expectations and commitments for the government and limits its capacity to deny services and to engage in strategies for cost containment. Despite such pressures, several countries are undertaking work to define core services more clearly or, alternatively, to establish expectations and guarantees regarding waiting times for treatment. In the Netherlands, some services have been delisted, and in New Zealand, new systems of assessment and prioritizing are being put in place for elective surgery, with the goal of making public entitlements more transparent.

CLASSIFYING HEALTH CARE SYSTEMS

No typology can easily classify different health care systems and reflect the diversity of public and private arrangements which are in force. One simple approach groups countries according to their financing systems, distinguishing countries which use public finance through general taxation (Australia, Canada, New Zealand, UK), public finance based on social insurance (Germany, Netherlands) and private finance, based on voluntary insurance or direct payments (United States). A related approach, used in OECD publications in 1992 and 1994, groups countries according to aspects of their systems of financing and delivery, as shown in Table 2.2.

Table 2.2 Public and private roles in health care systems

Country	Approach to funding and provision
Australia	Financed mainly by taxation with mixed public and private providers
Canada	Financed mainly by taxation with mainly private providers
Germany	Financed mainly by social insurance with mixed public and private providers
Netherlands	Financed by a mixture of social and private insurance, with mainly private providers
New Zealand	Financed mainly by taxation with mixed public and private providers
UK	Financed mainly by general taxation, with mainly public and private providers
United States	Financed mainly by voluntary insurance with mainly private providers

Source: OECD (1992, 1994)

In attempting to classify systems on the basis of their approach to payment and reimbursement systems, the OECD produced no less than eight possible system variants: two funding options (voluntary or compulsory), together with four options for paying providers (out-of-pocket by consumers, without insurance; out-of-pocket by consumers who are reimbursed; indirectly by third parties, via arm's-length contracts; and indirectly by third parties, via budgets and salaries within an integrated organization (OECD 1992). The study identified three broad systems: a private reimbursement model, with finance via compulsory or voluntary insurance with reimbursement of patients and no contracts between insurers and providers; a contract model with financing via compulsory social insurance or taxation and with contracts between insurers and providers; and an integrated model with compulsory finance through income-related contributions and/or general taxation, and with integration between funding/insurance and provision.

This taxonomy, developed by Jeremy Hurst (OECD 1992) was used to analyse the health systems of seven OECD countries and retained as a framework in a later study by Abel-Smith (OECD 1994) of the remaining 17 countries. The classification of real world health systems, making use of a simple taxonomy, proved to be difficult. Many health care systems are made up of different subsystems; for example involving contract systems for primary care and private hospitals, but integrated systems for hospitals. Moreover, the health reforms in the 1990s served to shift countries from one system type to another: for example, both the UK and New Zealand moved from the integrated model towards the contract model. Recent reforms have led to greater focus on the role of purchasers, yet purchasing has not featured within the system taxonomies.

Rather than presenting separate discussions of the systems, it was decided for this book to organize the seven countries into three groups. Countries in the first group, Germany and the Netherlands, share a traditional reliance on social insurance and a prominent role for private providers. The second group, the United States, Canada and Australia, are all federal systems involving public and private insurance; the US system funded primarily from voluntary private insurance. Countries in the third group, the UK and New Zealand, share features in terms of a reliance on tax funding, a substantial public sector role in the purchasing and provision of hospital services and the subsidization of primary care by GPs, who act as gatekeepers to secondary care. The two countries have also

followed similar reform patterns in terms of adopting a purchaser–provider split, thereby shifting from an integrated model to
a contract model.

In considering various ways of grouping the seven countries, it
became clear that the arrangements surrounding public and private
roles and interfaces are complex, and institutional arrangements
change over time. Each country has distinctive features as well as
attributes it shares with other countries.

3

ROLES AND INTERFACES: GERMANY AND THE NETHERLANDS

Both Germany and the Netherlands are examples of the 'Bismarck' social insurance system in which financing of health care is obtained from contributions by both employers and employees and comprehensive coverage is provided by both sickness funds and private insurers. The role of private insurance is much larger in the Netherlands than in Germany; however, both countries have been undertaking reforms which aim to increase competition among public and private insurers. The role of purchasing is not distinguished, and remains largely subsumed under that of funding or providing, or both. Traditionally, insurers were passive and exerted limited influence on the nature and quality of care delivered. Recent reforms have encouraged smarter purchasing. Only the Netherlands has arrangements for gatekeeping from the primary to the secondary care system.

As in many other European systems, there is considerable emphasis on universal coverage, and insurance schemes play an important redistributive role. Contributions are linked to an individual's ability to pay and not to health status, though some income groups can opt out and self-insure or insure privately. The health financing system is effective in redistributing among different age groups and income classes, between single individuals and families and between good and poor health risks, though redistribution is somewhat less than occurs within a universal tax-based financing system.

The systems in Germany and the Netherlands involve a corporatist approach to policy-making which requires governments to consult on policy changes with a large number of stakeholder groups. These groups include citizens, trade unions, employers, insurers and medical providers, among others. These requirements act as a constraint on the government's capacity to introduce and implement major system changes. In the late 1980s, a major set of reforms was proposed by the Dekker Commission. The proposals were not implemented as planned, though some changes have occurred. The reform design has attracted interest in international policy circles because of its potential to improve system performance across several health policy goals.

GERMANY

The German health care system utilizes a managed competition approach, and funds a mandated set of core services. The funding system was introduced by Chancellor Otto von Bismarck in 1883, and now covers 99 per cent of the population. Following the reunification of Germany in 1990, the East German health care system was reconfigured, over a five-year period, to align with that in the West. The system reflects the principles of solidarity and subsidiarity: solidarity leads to contribution rates that are linked to a person's ability to pay, while subsidiarity means that the state does not assume functions that can be performed as well or better by individuals, family or private self-governing organizations (Raffel and Raffel 1987; OECD 1992; Kamke 1997; Jost 1998; Ranade 1998).

Under the German constitution, responsibility for the health care system is shared. While the federal minister of health wields considerable power, *Länder* (states) also have important roles. The *Länder* supply human and physical capital for public health and hospitals, and fund medical education. They also own facilities, as do local governments and charities. While the federal government exerts a strong influence on the system, its key role is to regulate independent, statutory and semi-statutory health agencies. The government passes laws and issues guidelines for the financing and organization of health care. Then it withdraws, leaving funding, delivery and management of the health service to public and private organizations. An important characteristic of the system is the ineffective linkages between funders and providers of service.

The German health care system suffers organizational features which result in poor performance in terms of cost containment, efficiency and effectiveness, though gains have been made since the mid-1990s. Severe revenue problems arise from high rates of unemployment and the system's reliance on wage-based premiums as a revenue source. There is an oversupply of hospitals beds and physicians, poor integration across service providers and services, and high utilization rates and costs for pharmaceuticals and many other health care services (Jost 1998). Germany shares some problems with other European countries, including rising costs and pressures to adopt new technologies. Its demographic profile shows an ageing population, which will place upward pressure on future health care costs.

Public and private roles

Sources of funding for the German health care system are: payroll contributions 61 per cent, general taxation 11 per cent, private insurance 8 per cent, out-of-pocket payments 8 per cent, other social insurance 4 per cent, employers 4 per cent, private organizations 2 per cent (EOHCS 2000). There are three groups of insurers in the system: public insurance funds (called sickness funds, *RVO-kassen*, or state insurance regulation funds), substitute funds and private insurance funds.

The sickness funds are autonomous, non-profit insurers whose expenditures are constrained by the percentage of wages collected by each sickness fund. The funds act as third-party payers, reimbursing providers directly for preventative services, family planning, maternity care, prescription drugs, ambulatory medical care, dental care, transport, hospital inpatient care, and home nursing and rehabilitation services. They also pay for short-term income support when workers are unemployed owing to illness or accident. The funds must provide mandatory core services and can provide additional services, but are not responsible for the funding of nursing homes and retirement homes (OECD 1992).

The premium for the statutory sickness insurance funds is based on community rating, set at the same level for all members of a particular fund. As a result, premiums do not reflect an individual's risk factor, number of dependants, age, health status or services received but, rather, the average risk profile of all members of the scheme. The federal government mandates insurance coverage through public insurance funds for people below a certain income, the unemployed, retired people, self-employed farmers, disabled people, students and artists. Self-employed workers and civil servants are excluded from the statutory scheme. Workers enrol in public sickness funds (which cover 60 per cent of the population) according to their occupation, residence or employer, and their dependants are automatically covered. After retirement, fund members remain in their pre-retirement sickness fund (a national contribution rate is approximately 12–13 per cent).

Eighty-eight per cent of the population are covered by sickness funds. Seventy-five per cent of the population are mandatory members, and the balance includes voluntary members, whose income levels entitle them to opt out of the public system. The remaining 12 per cent of the population are either insured privately (9 per cent), have free access to health care (the armed forces, police and some social welfare recipients: 2 per cent), or have no health insurance but are wealthy (EOHCS 2000).

Public sickness funds cover 60 per cent of the population, while substitute funds cover 28 per cent of the population and allow companies to create their own alternative sickness funds for employees and their dependants. These national substitute funds, or *Ersatzkassen*, are still non-profit insurers, but they can charge lower premiums if they have a lower-risk membership. Unlike public funds, *Ersatzkassen* members govern substitute funds, which often reimburse providers at a higher rate than the statutory funds.

Private insurance companies provide services primarily to civil servants, the self-employed and high-income earners; however, only one-third of those eligible to choose private insurance do so. This occurs because the community-rated premiums of the statutory fund are lower than private insurance premiums for workers with a number of dependants and those who are high risk.

Private insurers charge members on the basis of an assessment of actuarial risk calculated to take account of the number, age and health profile of dependants. Premiums are calculated by dividing a person's expected lifetime expenses by the number of years that they are expected to belong to the insurance scheme. Thus, younger people tend to pay lower annual premiums because their longer membership period allows them to build up larger reserves for later care. This system provides disincentives for individuals to leave a private insurer, which are particularly strong for older people who must meet much higher premiums to compensate for a lack of reserves. Private insurers make indemnity payments in the form of cash reimbursements to members, as well as direct payments to providers (OECD 1992).

In 1995, 52 private health insurers operated in Germany, most being non-profit mutuals, but there were also 25 for-profit stock companies. The law regulates their fee schedules and premium calculations, though fees paid by private insurers are two to three times higher than those paid by sickness funds (Schulenburg and von der Graf 1994).

Private insurers provide supplementary insurance for approximately 8 per cent of the population. Supplementary insurance covers higher provider fees, access to prestigious specialists, and private hospital rooms. Once people opt out of the statutory insurance system, they cannot re-enter it. Employers must still pay half the premium if their employees choose private insurance, but only to the level required by statutory fund insurance. Civil servants receive a **reimbursement** from their employers of up to 80 per cent of the cost of private insurance.

Historically, the public insurance system offered very limited choice, and the minority who chose private insurance were discouraged from changing insurers, thus reducing the potential for competition among individual private insurance funds. However, since 1 July 1997, persons covered by statutory funds have been confronted with increased co-payments and a reduced benefits package but have greater choice of insurer. Individuals can now join the sickness fund of their choice, and terminate the contract if the sickness fund announces a contribution increase. This has led to the consolidation of sickness funds and, by 1999, the number of funds had fallen to less than 453, down from 1221 in 1993 (EOHCS 2000).

In Germany, decisions regarding what services are to be purchased are determined largely by the interactions of individuals with health care providers, though pressures exist because of global budget constraints. The insured select ambulatory physicians, and both providers and the insured decide the type of health care delivered. In the case of ambulatory care, the insurers bargain with regional associations of doctors, called the *Kassenärztliche Vereinigung* (KV), to determine prospective aggregate payments, and the KV then decides how to allocate funds to individual doctors. Negotiations take place under guidelines set by the Concerted Action Committee, a national representative body which agrees on maximum increases in health expenditures on ambulatory and dental care, pharmaceuticals and supplies. In general, insurer associations bargain with provider associations to set prospective overall budgets and the associations then reimburse the individual providers. Providers work in private practice, on a fee-for-service basis, within the budgetary allowance. The KV and insurers allocate points to every service; the points are then converted into Deutschmarks, based on the global budget. The KV pays individual doctors who must supply information on the number of points they have delivered. This system contains costs in that the value of a point is reduced if the global budget is exceeded. The global budget cap provides pressure on the system as it carries the threat of a lower price per service if volumes are exceeded. The KV also try to influence the number of services performed by profiling for each doctor the number of procedures per unit of time and per patient. However, without case review, judgements about the appropriateness of the volume of care cannot be made.

Patients are isolated from price information. Rather than paying directly, patients insured by the sickness funds receive vouchers, which they give to their doctors, and physicians then bill the sickness funds, though small-user part-charges may be imposed. Charges are subject to ceilings and exemptions exist for children and low-income recipients. There is limited consumer choice for hospital care, as usually patients must go to the nearest hospital.

Figure 3.1 presents the public expenditure on ambulatory care as a percentage of total health expenditure in the seven countries and shows Germany to have the highest percentage within the group. There are several reasons which contribute to the observed differences across countries. These include the tendency of some governments to concentrate public funding on secondary care; differences in the prices, quantities and volumes of primary and secondary care services; and variations in the kinds of service attracting public funding which are carried out in an ambulatory care setting. An important factor influencing the high percentage of Germany is the fact that the ambulatory system allows direct access to a wide range of specialists.

Funding for hospital care is also determined by bilateral negotiations between sickness funds (and private insurers) and individual hospitals, which may be publicly or privately owned. Historically, the two parties negotiated a prospective per diem reimbursement rate, regardless of the condition treated or type of treatment. Recent reforms have retained prospective payments but negotiate fees depending on the condition and treatment of the patient. This results in a **DRG-type prospective payment system**. Payments cover all aspects of care, except capital costs, which are seen to be the responsibility of government and charitable organizations. Additional money may be paid for certain high-cost procedures.

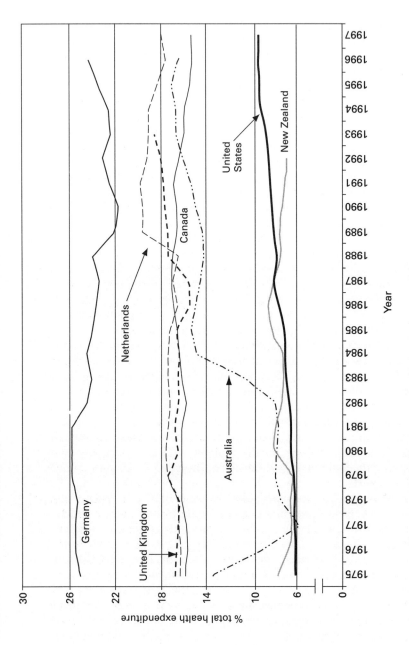

Figure 3.1 Public expenditure on ambulatory care in seven OECD countries, 1975–97
Source: OECD (1997)

In Germany, ambulatory doctors, with few exceptions, cannot treat patients in hospital; similarly, hospital doctors usually cannot see patients on an outpatient basis. This institutional demarcation has practical implications for funding arrangements and creates discontinuities in the care of patients. The ownership of hospitals and other health facilities spans both the public and private sectors. Professional regulation and constraints on health care organizations affect the level and nature of services received. Regulations also define the package of core services that must be offered by the insurers. Since whole services are either covered or not covered by insurance schemes, there are poor incentives to ensure that insured services give value for money. Funds have little incentive to provide services which do not comprise part of the core package.

Proposals for reform

There have been several efforts to reform the health care system in recent years. Since 1977, a number of cost-containment measures have been introduced to impose sectoral budget constraints on providers and pharmaceutical manufacturers, which have resulted in lower prices for certain brand-name products (Kamke 1997). Legislative measures were introduced in 1991 and 1993 which reduced reimbursement levels to providers. Provision was made for the new, compulsory nursing care insurance scheme to cover the costs of both home and hospital nursing care. The government imposed budget limitations on hospital, ambulatory and dental care and prescription drugs, and linked increases in budgets to the tax base of the sickness fund contributions.

Some reforms were aimed at curbing overprescription of drugs. For example, the 1993 budget for pharmaceuticals prescribed by ambulatory doctors was set at the 1991 level and, if the budget was exceeded, the first DM280 million was to be borne by provider associations. Specific reforms included an increase in co-payments, and the use of a list of preferred medicines for doctors and dentists, which required that the costs of medicines not on the list be charged to the pharmaceutical company or health care provider (Schulenburg and von der Graf 1994).

After 1996, a more market-oriented system based on capitation was introduced. Reform proposals focused on cost control involving measures such as replacing fee-for-service payments by capitation, replacing per diems by hospital cost diagnosis related groups

(DRGs) and patient management categories (PMCs), and restrictions on the ability of hospitals to make profits. Such measures have not only stimulated the growth of private hospitals, but also encouraged hospitals to cooperate with office-based practitioners. The reforms introduced in 1989 and 1993 yielded short-term cost reductions, but increases occurred in subsequent years. Reform strategies have tried to strengthen the self-governing capacity of insuring and providing organizations, with a view to stabilizing the contribution rate. Options for doing this included reductions to the scope of the basic benefits package and increases in patient co-payments. In 1997, increases in user charges were introduced which, although low, suggested that, in the future, up to one-third of the cost of health care might be met through co-payments and user charges.

The government has also introduced measures to allow the national committees of Statutory Health Insurers (SHI) physicians and SHI funds greater influence over the extent and nature of the benefits package. Where procedures do not meet certain criteria, it will be possible for SHI funds to offer them as optional services. Greater opportunities for innovation in the contracting of ambulatory care were opened up through the strategies of pilot projects and structural contracts, the latter allowing SHI physicians to establish a network of physicians who could act as budget-holders.

A particular difficulty within the system is the sharp separation between ambulatory and hospital care. Legislation passed in 1997 makes provision for local demonstration projects which could lead the way for greater emphasis on managed care as well as managed competition. There has been a fall in the length of stay in hospitals over recent years, though major increases in the number of GPs and specialists working outside the hospitals have helped to keep utilization rates high.

The 1997 reforms included a reduction in the sickness funds benefits package and also higher co-payments. The government lost its majority in the general election and, shortly thereafter, reforms were promised by a new government which was drawn from the Social Democratic and Green Parties. Reforms included a reduction in co-payments, an extension of benefits, and budgeting of expenditures on drugs, hospital care and out-patient care. The new government's Act to Strengthen Solidarity in SHI enabled these changes in 1998. Co-payments on pharmacists were lowered and spending caps were reintroduced. The Reform Act of SHI 2000 introduced a medium- to long-term reform whose key features are:

new processes and structures to strengthen health technology assessment with a view to improving efficiency and effectiveness; modifications which will allow contracts between sickness funds and providers, including incentives to encourage users to access specialists via their GP; and the introduction of new budget and reimbursement systems which will improve cost containment and efficiency.

System impacts

In other countries with a rich mixture of public and private insurers and providers, the phrase 'regulated' or 'managed' competition is used to describe governments' attempts to facilitate competition and contestability among public and private funders and providers. In Germany, the regulatory regime provides an obstacle to effective competition, at least in the form of price competition.

Efficiency

The German health care system scores poorly against the criterion of allocative efficiency. Getting the right level and mix of services at the margin is difficult since whole services are either covered or not covered by insurance schemes. There are poor incentives to ensure that the services provided are those that give value for money. Since the budgets of social insurance funds are closely linked to wage levels and not to the demand or need for medical services, resource utilization is largely related to macroeconomic and demographic variables.

The separate funding arrangements and responsibilities for public health, ambulatory and hospital care offer limited scope to make informed choices at the margin in terms of the level and mix of services. As a result, there is allegedly underfunding in areas like preventative care, public health programmes, psychiatric care and long-term care (OECD 1992). Limitations on the availability of care for the elderly and disabled appear to result in high levels of expenditure on acute hospital care.

While some efficiency gains have accompanied the move to prospective budgeting for hospital care on a per diem basis, this has led hospital administrators to make internal allocation decisions which place too much focus on personnel and health care production inputs, rather than on health outcomes.

There are various sources of technical inefficiency in the system.

Budget determination by bilateral decentralized negotiation processes does not support efficient purchasing. While KVs strongly organize physicians, sickness funds are less organized and thus in a weaker position to negotiate fees. In this situation, the monopoly power of providers outweighs the monopsony power of purchasers to control fees and contain costs.

Ambulatory doctors have incentives to overservice patients and to maximize throughput for monetary gain. While the level of subsidy is reduced if specified volumes are exceeded, there is little information available to each doctor to inform them about aggregate service levels. The segmentation of ambulatory and hospital services is a source of inefficiency and can result in diagnostic procedures being repeated once a patient is admitted to hospital.

Most doctors are in sole practice, although there are some partnerships of two doctors in the same speciality. This may lead to poor case management, which could be improved if there were more multispeciality practices. The system appears to have a serious oversupply of doctors (estimated at 15,000 unemployed doctors) and a shortage of nurses. The oversupply acts to increase utilization rates and maintain the role of doctors in delivering services that could be produced more efficiently by nurses.

By 1998, the medical workforce was 4 per cent less than its peak in 1995. The preventative and rehabilitative workforce had also decreased by 10 per cent from its peak in 1996. Between 1991 and 1998 the average length of a hospital stay decreased by 24 per cent (western parts) and 35 per cent (eastern parts) and average stays fell by 15 per cent (western parts) and 18 per cent (eastern parts) in the preventative and rehabilitative institutions.

The direct payment of providers by physician associations reduces administrative costs, although the large number of small sickness funds raises costs. Administration costs were 15.5 per cent of total contributions of health expenditure in 1992 for private insurers, compared to 0.9 per cent in the UK, and 12.7 per cent in Australia (Behrens 1997; AIHW 1998). Germany's proportion of health expenditure on administration is the highest of the seven countries studied.

Cost containment

The German reforms have encountered obstacles in their efforts to achieve cost containment and greater efficiency. These include legal impediments to closer, more effective linkages between insurers and providers, and also, limited policy focus, arising from the diffusion of state monopsony power and decision-making between the federal and state levels.

Cost-containment objectives are difficult to achieve because of the split of responsibilities among the central state, the federal *Länder* and corporatist institutions such as sickness funds' associations on the purchasing side and physicians' and dentists' associations on the providing side. Germany's success in cost containment at the ambulatory care level can be traced to the responsibilities of provider associations to deliver a full range of specialist services within a fixed budget. In contrast, hospital cost control has been problematic since hospitals contract individually with the sickness funds, reducing their potential to exert monopsony power over providers (Schwartz and Busse 1997: 107).

Financing arrangements have not achieved a good matching between prices and costs. For example, when compulsory nursing care insurance was introduced in 1995, private insurance companies agreed to make the cover available to those currently receiving nursing care, but were not allowed to adjust premiums to reflect individual risk. Although private insurers responded by establishing a pool to distribute the burden among themselves, further problems arose when the demand for service greatly exceeded the total revenues available.

Equity

The principles of universality and solidarity create a health system which provides all citizens with universal access to a core of affordable health care. Equity problems arise, however, from the autonomous and self-funding nature of sickness funds, which leads to differences in benefit levels across funds. Statistics on enrolment figures demonstrate that blue-collar workers are heavily represented in statutory funds, white-collar workers in substitute funds and civil servants in private insurance schemes. Yet the inverse care law suggests that low-income workers are likely to have the highest demands for services (Navarro 1991).

Data on provider incomes suggests that those who are insured by substitute and private insurers get better access to services than those insured by statutory funds. Substitute and private insurers pay higher fees for services, which represents an incentive for providers to service this group. One estimate suggests that at a time when private insurers covered only 6–8 per cent of people, they generated about 20 per cent of physician incomes (Navarro 1991: 567). As greater competition has been encouraged among insurance funds, there have been concerns that insurance companies will try to shed high risks. In an effort to offset this, new policies to introduce free choice of insurer have been accompanied by provisions which require insurance funds with low-risk populations to subsidize funds with high-risk populations.

Choice

Patients are free to choose their ambulatory physicians but have more limited choice of hospital care. Individuals have always had a wide choice among specialist providers. Traditionally, those on higher incomes had opportunities to shop for insurers, though recent reforms have extended choices regarding insurers to others.

The move to encourage stronger links between insurers and providers will also serve to reduce consumer choice of provider by introducing health maintenance organization (HMO) and preferred provider organization (PPO) type arrangements involving managed care. Lower premiums are being offered, so long as patients are willing to allow GPs to act as gatekeepers to specialist services.

Despite new freedoms to enter and exit insurance systems, patients have limited information and influence over the care they receive. This suggests that consumer choice could be enhanced through greater access to information regarding the net benefits of health care interventions and alternative insurance arrangements.

Conclusion

Germany is at a crossroads in health care reform. Its laws and public policies governing the health care funding and provider systems are complex, and responsibilities are largely divested to other organizations. The tight caps placed on operating budgets and control of capital have increased the rationing of services. Some suggest that Germany is facing a political paralysis not dissimilar to that which blocked the United States' attempts at reform (Jost 1998). The system is hampered by laws and regulations which pose impediments to competition, and limit reform strategies which promote cost containment and efficiency.

Future health policy reforms will continue to focus on the goal of cost containment. It is still unclear whether Germany will move towards a full-blown model of managed competition, with its wide diversity of funding options, or create a highly regulated public sickness fund aimed at increasing the government's monopsony purchasing role. Reform discussions surrounding sickness funds tend to focus on HMO- and PPO-type models, which will limit the ability of individuals to choose their physicians and allow funds to negotiate contracts with hospitals and physicians. Insurers need better information to assist them in purchasing cost-effective health care to improve health outcomes. They need to contract directly with providers, have greater scope to differentiate their products and be able to inform potential consumers about trade-offs between risk and price.

Recent measures to promote competitiveness among insurers will provide stronger incentives for the selection of low-risk clients (called 'raisin-picking' in the German context). Though providers wish to maintain their independence, this must be balanced against the desire of insurers to shift costs and to target cost containment measures rather than efficiency. If the insurers align their objectives strategically with those of providers, this could disadvantage high-risk individuals seeking insurance cover. It is likely that elements of managed care (by this or other names) and managed competition will feature in any proposals likely to make real improvements in the efficiency and cost containment of the German system.

THE NETHERLANDS

Expenditure on health care in the Netherlands was 8.9 per cent of GDP in 1996 and the health system is regarded as performing well in terms of standards of care. In the late 1980s a set of proposals for health reform based on a strategy of managed (regulated) competition was recommended by the Committee on the Structure and Financing of Health Care (the Dekker Committee), a government-appointed advisory committee. The proposals were not implemented in full, and were modified over a series of years. In some cases, behavioural change occurred in anticipation of legislation which was never put in place. The reform design remains of international interest because of its potential to improve performance in relation to the policy goals of efficiency, cost containment, equity and choice.

Public and private roles

Funding for health care in the Netherlands places reliance on health insurance, and a compulsory social insurance scheme exists for long-term care. Insurance for the services of physicians and hospitals is provided by a mixture of mandatory sickness fund insurance and private insurance. Approximately two-thirds of the population are mandated to purchase insurance, and approximately one-third of the population (whose incomes are above a ceiling) can opt out. However, participation in voluntary private health insurance is very high, resulting in 99 per cent of the population being insured. Employers make contributions to health insurers on behalf of their employees. Payments to the sickness funds are income-related and, in addition, individuals pay a small fee. While sickness funds originally operated regionally, they have been subject to amalgamation and rationalization, and funds now operate nationally.

In 1998, sources of funding for health care were: sickness fund insurance (ZFW) 33 per cent, long-term care (AWBZ) 36 per cent, private health insurance 15 per cent, direct payments 9 per cent, and government taxes 5 per cent (Okma 1997). While contributions to social insurance are based on income, private insurance policy-holders pay fixed premiums and also make out-of-pocket payments for services received. Employers subsidize public and private insurance for their employees on the same basis. Private insurers normally reimburse the patient for fees paid to providers.

In 1998, expenditure on health care was DFl 66.5 billion, DFl 27.3 billion for hospitalization, DFl 12.0 billion for institutional care and DFl 27.2 billion for doctor and dentist consultations and medicines (Okma 1997). The country has an extensive system of primary health care which is structured around GPs and community nurses. GPs and most specialists are self-employed and about half of GPs work in group practices or health centres. Nearly all primary care is provided to patients by their GPs, who also act as gatekeepers to specialists and hospitals. Specialists usually work within hospitals, although some have independent practices.

Government planning laws can limit the numbers of both family doctors and specialists, and physician incomes are also subject to negotiation. Indicators reveal that the Netherlands has relatively low physician consultation rates, very low prescribing rates, a relatively low acute hospital admission rate and a relatively high average length of stay in acute hospitals. The number of physicians and acute beds per capita are comparable with those of other OECD countries (OECD 1992). About 85 per cent of government-regulated care is delivered by private, non-profit institutions, and government provision occurs particularly in the area of acute hospital care. Though the Dutch per capita physician expenditure is half the European average and one-quarter of the US level, there are concerns about the effects of technology advances and an ageing population (Jackson 1996).

Public health services are financed through general taxation and managed in a regional setting by municipalities. Domiciliary health services are generally provided by the 'Cross' organizations, and financed jointly by the exceptional medical expenses fund and by direct client payments.

Physician remuneration varies for GPs and specialists, and the level is influenced by the type of insurance the patient holds. Privately insured patients and public employees can consult any GP they wish, on a fee-for-service basis. The patients then claim back the fees from their insurers, which are set according to a national schedule. For patients enrolled in sickness funds, GPs are paid on a capitation basis by the funds (Kirkman-Liff and van de Ven 1989).

Specialists are generally paid on a fee-for-service basis, for both privately and publicly insured patients. Patients are given referral cards entitling them to specialist treatment for one month, but specialists are paid over and above this by fee-for-service for an extensive list of diagnostic and therapeutic procedures (OECD 1992). Specialists decide their own fees, the total amount of which is compared each year to the norm income for specialists. Those exceeding this standard must reimburse a share of income above this level. The measures act as a check on the tendency for physicians to increase the volume of services in order to increase their incomes.

National physician and insurer bodies negotiate capitation rates and fees within limits set by government regulation. This process is complex, with separate negotiations for the personal income of physicians and for the reimbursement of practice expenses. For sickness fund patients, the payment level is derived by adding the negotiated norm income and norm practice costs, and then dividing by the norm patient volume to arrive at the monthly capitation rate. For privately insured patients, the fee schedule is based on prices fixed for the type of visit.

The government has strong control over hospital expansion and activities, and remunerates hospitals on the basis of annual prospective global budgets (Lapré 1988). Prior to 1988, global hospital budgets were based on historical costs, but this system tended to penalize more efficient hospitals. It was also characterized by cost-shifting strategies that promoted off-budget services beyond the control of regulations (Robinson 1997). From 1988, the budget allocation formula has been set with the aim of making the cost of functions and services equivalent across acute hospitals. This system of budget allocation allows money to follow the patient since changes to catchment populations and service volumes are reflected in budget changes, settled at the annual budget negotiations.

Over the 1990s there has been evidence of greater horizontal and vertical integration of health care and health insurance services. Boundaries between hospital and ambulatory care are softening and there is a shift from inpatient to ambulatory care.

Proposals for reform

The Dekker Committee's proposals called for the establishment of competitive markets in health care and health insurance which would remove existing distinctions between the sickness funds and private insurers. The objective was to provide greater equity by universal access to a standard package of core services and to improve efficiency through the creation of a more competitive market for health insurance and health care. The resulting system, based on the concept of health vouchers, provided scope for the achievement of both efficiency and equity goals.

Individuals would pay compulsory income-related contributions into a central fund for basic insurance which would make risk-adjusted capitation payments to competing private and public insurers. In addition, individuals could facilitate access to services beyond the core through the purchase of supplementary insurance. The reforms proposed that capitation payments covered 85 per cent of the premium, and the remaining 15 per cent be paid by individuals on a voluntary flat-rate basis. Arising from the public good attributes of public health services, funding would be maintained within the government budget, and not assigned to competing health insurers.

The proposals required the government to introduce regulations to foster a competitive market environment, including the power to fix the income-related basic insurance premium, define the basic insurance package, and guarantee open enrolment to all insurance funds. This system of regulated (managed) competition was designed to enhance the competitiveness of health insurance and health care markets and replace direct government involvement in the setting of volumes and prices for health services. The proposals involved replacing the four-part network of insurance plans with a uniform compulsory scheme of basic national health insurance for all Dutch residents. Integration of health care with related social care was a key component of the reforms. Individuals would have free choice of insurer, and insurers would be required to accept all applicants for cover, in the interests of equity and access. Policyholders would be free to change insurers if they wished and could purchase supplementary insurance to cover services outside the core. Insurers were not allowed to discriminate against high-risk individuals and were required to charge the same premium to all policyholders under the same plan (Ministry of Welfare, Health and Cultural Affairs 1988: 69). Figure 3.2 portrays the health system as envisaged under the Dekker reforms.

The reforms aimed to empower health consumers relative to providers of care, including measures to underscore patients' rights, extend complaint procedures and fund organizations to provide information to consumers. The state would maintain oversight over the quality of care and regulate the health insurance system (Ministry of Welfare, Health and Cultural Affairs 1988). In developing the reform proposals, the government was concerned about possible adverse selection through cream-skimming if too much risk was placed on the sickness funds (van de Ven 1997).

The Dekker proposals attracted considerable international attention and inspired reform proposals in New Zealand in the early 1990s. An attractive feature of the reform design was its ability to achieve improvements across a number of public policy goals. Equity was promoted by tax funding, together with income-testing and risk-rating, which guaranteed access to a state-mandated core. Varying the size of the voucher linked premiums to the level of risk being insured, and promoted efficiency in private insurance markets by compensating insurers for higher-risk groups. Price competition among insurers and the need for individuals to contribute promoted allocative and technical efficiency, and also cost containment. Individuals were given choice of insurer for basic care and also the opportunity to purchase supplementary private insurance.

Gradual implementation of the reforms began in early 1989, but was suspended with the change of government in November 1989. Following a review, the broad thrust of the reforms was maintained. It was renamed the Simons Plan, after the new secretary for health, and placed less emphasis on the role of competition and markets. The new package extended the financial coverage of the basic

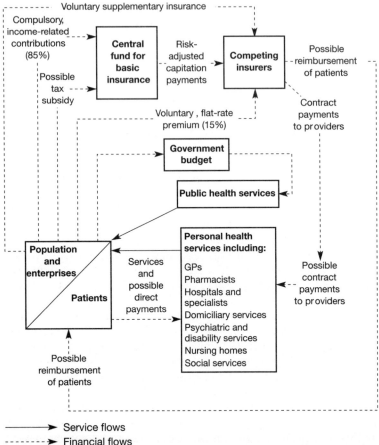

Service flows
Financial flows

Figure 3.2   The health and the social care system in the Netherlands
following the Dekker reforms
Source: OECD (1992)

insurance package (from 85 per cent to 97 per cent); changed the
ratio between the compulsory, income-based part of the basic insurance premium and the negotiable flat-rate part from 75/25 to 85/15;
restricted the provision of basic insurance to non-profit insurers;
and introduced more competition between sickness funds (OECD
1992). Further modifications were made in 1995 resulting in two
different regulatory regimes: regulated competition for the basic

insurance package (which covered hospital and physician services) and direct government regulation with respect to planning, budgeting and prices in areas such as nursing home care and long-term institution care. The government decided to remove legal regulations concerning hospital budgeting and to place greater reliance on competition among insurers as a strategy for keeping health costs down.

While the Dekker reforms were not implemented as originally conceived, changes occurred which made the health system more sensitive to market forces. This happened particularly in the area of the sickness funds, which became more competitive. As of the mid-1990s, the sickness funds received risk-adjusted capitation payments based on age, sex, region and disability but were responsible for only 3 per cent of the difference between actual and predicted expenses. The government made clear, however, that its long-term intention was to increase the level of responsibility of sickness funds from 3 to 100 per cent, apart from fixed hospital costs. This will not only increase pressures on the funds to become efficient purchasers but will also provide them with stronger incentives to 'cream skim'.

The funding environment for sickness funds is now more competitive in several ways: the operation of sickness funds has been opened up to private insurers; sickness funds can now contract selectively with physicians and pharmacists; and sickness fund members can now choose among different funds at least every two years. Competition among sickness funds has grown based on their level of flat-rate premiums, reputation and service quality (Robinson 1997). Plans have also been announced to increase the financial risk for private insurers, especially for persons over 65, to regulate premium levels, and to ensure open enrolment. As the market for insurance becomes more competitive, strategies will be required to equalize risk among insurance pools or, alternatively, to compensate those who insure groups with higher risk profiles. It is anticipated that, over time, the differences between sickness funds and private insurance will disappear.

System impacts

While the Dekker–Simons proposals were not implemented in full, the rationale for reform can be seen in terms of the expected improvements to performance against specific health policy goals.

Efficiency

The pre-reform health care system contained few incentives for efficient behaviour on the part of providers, insurers or patients. Patients insured by sickness funds were not made aware of the costs of care received, and funds had poor incentives and limited capacity to restrict demand (OECD 1992). Public and private insurers operated within a financing system offering little reward for efficiency. Sickness funds were reimbursed from a general fund for all realized claims expenses, so they had no financial incentive to select efficient providers. If the fund did improve the efficiency of its operations, it received less revenue from the General Fund (Kirkman-Liff and van de Ven 1989: 38). Furthermore, the sickness funds were required to contract with any local provider wishing to offer services to the funds' members, thus making them passive funders of care. Private insurers, while being aware of costs, found it more profitable to compete by cream-skimming good risks than by choosing cost-effective providers of care, given the existing premium structure (Kirkman-Liff and van de Ven 1989).

The complexity of the financing and insurance system created barriers to selecting those services which were most effective at improving health outcomes. Providers of care operated in a system that resulted in widespread inefficiencies. Incorrect price signals were frequently sent to users and providers as prices and fees were set either by government regulations or by government-approved negotiations between providers and insurers. Prices did not reflect real costs and thus gave misleading information regarding efficiency (van de Ven 1990a; Robinson 1997).

GPs were paid on a fee-for-service basis for their privately insured patients, and this did not dissuade them from providing unnecessary care. Although GPs were paid by capitation for services provided to sickness-fund patients, this sometimes created allocative inefficiencies when GPs decided to refer patients to specialists rather than providing the treatment themselves (Kirkman-Liff and van de Ven 1989).

Prior to recent reforms the institutional health arrangements promoted increasing volumes of secondary care treatments, as there were no limits on treatment volumes, and discretion was left to the practitioner to prescribe care. The Dekker Committee found fault with the hospital system for the lack of cost-consciousness among physicians, stating that many examinations were routine and were of limited utility (Ministry of Welfare, Health and Cultural Affairs 1988). Specialists were remunerated on a fee-for-service basis, so that they received income for unnecessary as well as necessary care (OECD 1992).

Policy reforms which have increased competitive pressures on insurers and providers have provided stronger incentives for efficiency. Under regulated competition, insurers are free to choose whether or not they contract with providers: the onus is on the providers efficiently and effectively to supply health care (Robinson 1997). Insurers, and ultimately their policyholders, have the power to ensure that providers meet their requirements (like the price and quality of care) by threatening to withhold or withdraw contracts (Lapré 1988).

The administrative costs of private health insurers are notably higher than those of centralized sickness funds (Schut and van de Ven 1987) and the introduction of regulated competition leads to an increase in the administrative costs of processing and monitoring claims. However, efficiency cannot be measured only by administrative costs, but must assess the overall impact of reforms on allocative and technical efficiency. It was estimated that introduction of the Dekker reforms had the potential to make savings of up to 15 per cent of total health care expenditures (Kirkman-Liff and van de Ven 1989: 38).

Cost containment

The Dutch health care system has had ongoing difficulties with cost containment, though system changes have brought some improvements. The hospital funding allocation formula eliminated some of the historical inefficiencies of the global budget system established in 1983. The new global budget system was an improvement over the old practice as physicians' incomes were checked in a number of ways, including regulation through negotiations between insurer and physician associations, with the result that they rose at a slower rate than the consumer price index. Effective caps on physician income forced specialists to repay income earned that surpassed their norm income.

Sickness funds were able now to assimilate comprehensive data on physician services, and physicians were not paid unless the information was supplied. The funds processed these data in order to compile national averages, which were used to compare physicians within regions and nationwide. Voluntary peer review programmes were established, and physicians with above-average rates were singled out.

The system of reimbursements to pharmacists for drug dispensing services was consciously structured with cost containment and efficiency in mind. Starting in 1999, pharmacists received a bonus for dispensing cheaper medicines, on top of the fixed mark-up they received per prescribed medicine. Sickness funds reduced entitlements in areas such as eyeglasses, physiotherapy and over-the-counter drugs. Certain co-payments and co-insurance measures were introduced in an attempt to promote efficiency. Efforts were made to promote a sense of ownership and more responsible behaviour by individuals with a view to keeping costs down and minimizing premiums and co-payments (Okma 1998: 3–4). Greater focus on disease management provided incentives to move care from institutional to community settings.

Equity

The Dutch health care system has always been regarded as providing equitable access to care. An acknowledged feature of the system is the high standard of care, medical knowledge and technology. Care facilities are evenly distributed and easily accessible, and emphasis is placed on health protection and promotion. Most of the basic insurance is financed from an income-based premium, independent of age and health status, which accords with an equitable ability-to-pay principle. The flat-rate premium paid directly by the insured to the insurer must be the same for each individual under the same insurance plan. Also, insurers are legally obligated to accept all applicants for cover to ensure accessibility. Despite this, the Dekker–Simons reform proposals were challenged on equity. Questions were raised about the reduced involvement of the government in the sector, and about the affordability of the insurance premiums. Concerns were expressed that if procedures used to classify risk groups were too crude, that cream-skimming could still occur (Zweifel and Frech 1992).

Choice

Patients covered under private insurance and the public service scheme have totally free choice of GP, whereas patients insured under a sickness fund are limited in their choice of practitioner to those who hold contracts. Choice is limited to the practitioners and institutions in that region, but this restriction does not apply to teaching hospitals, tuberculosis sanatoria or mental hospitals. It is also possible for insurers to approve treatment for patients from GPs or institutions not contracted to their sickness funds, or in municipalities outside the region where the patient lives (Ministry of Welfare, Health and Cultural Affairs 1988: 13).

The GP chosen by a patient takes responsibility for the patient's primary care and controls all referrals to specialists and hospitals. Patients are allowed to choose their specialists after they are referred by their GP (Kirkman-Liff and van de Ven 1989: 37). However, all patients face choice constraints resulting from a lack of information about the quality of care, prices, waiting lists and other relevant matters.

Traditionally, patient choice of insurer was circumscribed and those individuals covered by the sickness funds generally had little choice about their insurer since most funds were monopolies operating in a legally defined geographical area. Public sector employees were required to join compulsory insurance schemes. Individuals who were able to opt out of the public schemes had greater choice since they could seek cover for non-exceptional risks from one of many proprietary and non-profit private health insurers (OECD 1992: 90–1).

Conclusion

The Dutch health sector is on a path to implementing regulated competition between sickness funds and private insurers in the area of non-catastrophic risks. If choice of insurer is to be offered, then the government will need to ensure that adequate risk-adjusted mechanisms are put in place. Risk adjustment is essential to encouraging sickness funds and private insurers to compete on the basis of efficiency rather than by cream-skimming. These reforms will promote further improvements to the quality and efficiency of purchasing decisions in the markets for health insurance and health care and will strengthen linkages between funders and providers.

Policy challenges have resulted from the combination of collective arrangements for income protection and private sector dominance in the administration, management and ownership of the health care system. One suggestion is that policy-making processes are suffering from erosion in the neocorporatist social 'middle ground' between governments and private organizations (van der

Grinten, 1996). The Dutch government has introduced changes to the number of advisory committees and consultative processes in an effort to soften the impact of interest groups on the reform process (Okma 1997: 9). The diffuse nature of political power, the level of professional autonomy and the power of insurers have served to constrain health sector reform.

4

ROLES AND INTERFACES: UNITED STATES, CANADA AND AUSTRALIA

The United States, Canada and Australia are countries in which the health care system spans different levels of government, and complex arrangements arise from the split of responsibilities for funding, purchasing and provision within a federal system. System features vary across states and provinces making it difficult to offer a simple description of the health care system which is in force. Canada and the United States share geographical proximity and a common inheritance, since prior to the adoption of universal insurance in 1971, Canada's system resembled that in the United States. Australia shifted from reliance on private insurance to a universal public system drawing on the experiences of Canada. Over the years, the systems have evolved in ways which have led to major shifts to the roles and interfaces of public and private organizations.

The countries have developed diverse system features and approaches to reform. Their policy debates and experiences provide rich opportunities for learning about policy choices surrounding public and private roles and interfaces. All three countries share deep concerns about the sustainability of public and total system costs. In Australia, concerns about the government's fiscal risk have led to the adoption of tax subsidies to encourage the purchase of private insurance. Fiscal problems in Canada have challenged the government's long-standing commitment to a universal single-tier system. In the United States, the Clinton health reforms were not successful in introducing a universal insurance approach, leading instead to piecemeal reforms at the state level, driven primarily by the private sector and involving elements of both managed competition and managed care.

The predominance of private providers in the three countries means that health professionals have power and influence over the system. The history of reform has shown that attempts at direct confrontation with the medical profession are often unsuccessful from a government point of view. Moves towards managed care and limitations of the clinical practice of professions imposes strains, and has led to new relationships being formed between managed care organizations and the health professions. The success of public policies is influenced by the degree of support for them that can be obtained by health professionals. While, in Canada, health authorities have considerable control over professional fees, such interventions in Australia would be ruled unconstitutional and regarded as civil conscription.

UNITED STATES

The United States spends more on health care than any other OECD country. During the 1990s, expenditures grew annually, both as a percentage of GDP and in real terms. Health expenditures accounted for 14 per cent of GDP in 1998 and projected levels for 2005 are as high as 18 per cent (Weil 1996: 269; Dowd and Tilson 1998). Despite the quantum of resources devoted to health care, the United States does not enjoy better health outcomes as measured by mortality rates and other indicators.

The escalating cost of health care has generated the impetus for reforming the health care system, though major changes have been difficult to achieve. The system suffers from a lack of central regulation and the dominating influence of competition and private markets (Shalala and Reinhardt 1999).

Public and private roles

The US health care system comprises multitudinous private and public arrangements in the areas of funding, purchasing and provision. Individual and employer responsibilities for funding dominate the system, i.e. there is no universal health care system, and the government's role is more limited than in other systems. Health care funding is a mixture of federal, state and local insurance, private insurance paid for or subsidized by employers, and out-of-pocket payments. Purchasing is undertaken by employers, third-party payers (such as the federal and state governments), insurance companies, health maintenance organizations (HMOs) and doctors. Financial arrangements in the United States range from traditional private indemnity insurance based on fee-for-service care, to managed care arrangements, involving varying degrees of risk-sharing among parties. The complexity and diversity of health care approaches limit the scope for central coordination and planning of health care services at the federal and state levels.

In 1996, 46.7 per cent of health spending was financed by government sources (Medicare 19.6 per cent, Medicaid 14.3 per cent and other government programmes 12.8 per cent), and 53.3 per cent by the private sector (16.5 per cent out-of-pocket, 32.6 per cent private insurance and 4.2 per cent other private). Private health insurance dominates funding arrangements in the United States and approximately three-quarters of the population is covered by private health insurance, which is obtained via an employer (61 per cent) or directly (13 per cent). This insurance is offered by more than a thousand companies which are partly regulated by the individual states. State regulation requires that certain benefits are mandatory for all companies operating within a state.

Approximately 43 million individuals, equivalent to 18.3 per cent of Americans under the age of 65, are uninsured (Gold 1999: 5). Lack of insurance reflects employment status and also problems of affordability. Failure of the Clinton reforms halted moves towards universal coverage and has led to further growth in the number of uninsured. Those who lack insurance obtain health care at 50–70 per cent of the level received by an average insured person (Gold 1993: 24). Specific services for the uninsured are sometimes available through federal, state and local government health clinics and hospitals. Care for the uninsured is subsidized indirectly by those who purchase health insurance. Providers also subsidize the uninsured, though prospective payment systems have reduced their capacity to treat, and itemized billing has made it more difficult to build in extra costs.

In 1996, approximately 34.7 per cent of total health expenditure was for hospital care, 19.5 per cent physician services, 7.6 per cent for nursing home care, 25.9 per cent for other personal care, 3 per cent on research and construction, and 9.3 per cent on all other care. Price is important to employers and individuals in determining the choice of health care cover. Employer-provided insurance is often substituted for wages since it is tax exempt. Policies differ enormously, and while larger industries provide extensive coverage, some service industries tend to purchase bottom-line insurance policies which cover only ambulatory care. Premiums are experience-rated for companies and the key determinants of premium levels include company size and the type of employment. Large companies are able to negotiate better deals than small ones, and the employees' share of premium varies. Low-income people in small businesses generally pay a higher share of their premiums.

There can be several hundred insurers operating in a given region. Generally, between three and twelve insurers are the significant purchasers for any given provider. These groups have the bargaining power, while the individual and other small payers having very little say (Tiesberg *et al.* 1994: 133). Providers must monitor and be aware of what insurers are willing to cover. There has been a growing trend of mergers between individuals and small employer-based groups, with a view to pooling risk and increasing buying power. Some companies have found ways to reduce their costs by self-insuring employee health expenses. Self-insuring reduces the companies' exposure to state regulations for health insurance and limits the amount they must pay out for specific conditions, though in practice, this has been challenged in the courts. More than half of all group insurance company coverage is provided by self-insurance (OECD 1994).

Insurance comes in many forms including co-insurance, stop-loss with a limit on cover, deductible costs of specified amounts, and specific coverage for such treatment as pharmaceuticals and in/out-patient care. The cost is experience-rated, and variables taken into account include age, type of employment and health status. Insurance is also provided through managed care arrangements. A majority of privately insured Americans are enrolled in managed care plans that limit choice of doctors and treatments (Eckholm 1994).

Virtually all Americans 65 years and older receive public coverage through Medicare which is the largest health insurer in the country. Medicare also insures the permanently disabled and people with end-stage renal disease. It is divided into parts A and B. Part A is financed by payroll taxes (equal shares from employers and employees) and covers hospital services, some nursing home care and home health services. Medicare beneficiaries are charged a first day deductible for in-patient treatment. Part B is optional. About 95 per cent of eligible people enrol by paying a premium, entitling them to insurance cover for physicians' services, outpatient hospital care and ambulatory care (Raffel and Raffel, in Raffel 1997: 8). The premium contributes 25 per cent of costs, and federal government revenues make up the rest. As Medicare pays for less than half the medical expenses incurred by beneficiaries, many recipients (70 per cent) also purchase supplementary insurance.

Medicaid, a joint federal and state health insurance programme, is also available for targeted groups of poor. These groups include the aged, blind, disabled, pregnant and the parent(s) of dependent children. States define maximum income and asset levels for eligibility to the programme. The federal government matches state payments at rates that vary by state personal income levels. The range of the federal share is from 50 to 83 per cent. Medicaid also provides cover for preventative, acute and long-term care.

Federal and state public employees also have their own health benefit programmes, the largest of which is the Federal Employees Health Benefit Program (FEHBP), as does the military. The Civilian Health and Medical Program of the Uniform Services (CHAMPUS) was established to guarantee military personnel free medical care for their entire life, and allowed spouses and dependent children free medical care when spare capacity existed. The military was faced with escalating costs akin to those in the civilian health system and responded by establishing managed care schemes in partnership with military facilities. Tricare, launched in 1995, and providing three levels of coverage, has helped curb the escalation of military health expenditure and improved the quality of care, but access problems have been experienced (Minton 1996).

With the exception of Mcdicaid, people often need more than one insurance policy because of the lack of integration between acute and long-term care provisos in insurance policies. Premiums have been increasing despite strong competition within the insurance market. This has pushed many employers to downgrade to bottom-line policies that have little long-term coverage. Small firms of fewer than 50 people have been affected by premium increases because insurance companies see them as a high **actuarial risk**. There has been a dramatic increase in secondary policies and out-of-pocket payments made by employees in an effort to maintain adequate levels of coverage.

Managed care from HMOs and preferred provider organizations (PPOs) provides coordinated care. Health maintenance organizations work on the basis that people pay a fixed enrolment fee for a comprehensive benefit package which can only be provided by an HMO-sanctioned practitioner or facility. PPOs differ in that they selectively contract with doctors, hospitals and other providers to obtain services at a discounted fee. More recently, the point of service (POS) networks have been developed. These networks extend an HMO to include a PPO component, so they can allow some freedom of choice for providers and at the same time contain costs (OECD 1994: 324).

As of the mid-1980s, the government owned 25 per cent of general short-term hospital beds; non-profit organizations owned 65 per cent, and the remaining 10 per cent were privately owned. Non-profit hospitals are usually run by community or religious groups with an elected board of trustees at the helm. In the late 1980s, significant corporatization of hospitals occurred and this promoted a proliferation of for-profit facilities. Providers of the health services are increasingly owned by big business. 'Combined with the ... pharmaceutical deals, health care mergers surpassed in value those of any other industry for 1994' (Eckholm 1994). Short-term hospital care is mainly provided by non-profit and government-run facilities.

Table 4.1 provides selected statistics on aspects of health care provision across the seven OECD countries. It demonstrates the much higher levels of service utilization which characterize the US system and, in particular, the reliance on diagnostic testing through magnetic resonance imaging (MRI) and computerized tomography (CT) techniques.

While many physicians are self-employed, some own diagnostic facilities such as imaging, and physical therapy units. In this situation, providers and purchasers may be the same entities, and the overproduction of services is more problematic in physician-owned facilities. Managed care arrangements and legislative and regulatory changes have been introduced in an effort to reduce costs and improve efficiencies in an increasingly competitive market (Aday et al. 1993: 111). One example of this is 1992 legislation which forbids physicians from billing Medicare patients for services performed in laboratories in which the doctor has a direct financial interest (Tiesberg et al. 1994: 136).

In the United States, many doctors operate as specialists: 85 per cent of practising physicians have specialty credentials (Roemer 1991a: 108) General practitioner gross earnings are high compared with other OECD countries, contributing to high physician expenditure per capita. General practitioners' incomes are considerably

Table 4.1 Hospital spending and selected characteristics in seven countries, 1996

Country	Per capita spending on hospitals[a]	Percentage of total health spending on hospitals	Percentage of population admitted	Average length of stay (days)	MRI units per million population	CT scanners per million population
Australia	767	43.2	13.8	15.5	2.9	18.4[c]
Canada	918	44.5	12.5	10.5	1.3[b]	7.9[b]
Germany	796	35.0	20.7	14.3	5.7	16.4
Netherlands	954	53.4	11.1	32.5	3.9[b]	9.0[d]
New Zealand	573	45.1	14.1	6.5	2.7	7.7
UK	521[b]	42.0	23.0	9.8	3.4[b]	6.3[d]
United States	1646	42.2	12.4	7.8	16.0[b]	26.9[d]
Average	882	43.6	15.37	13.8	5.1	13.2

[a]adjusted using purchasing power parities; [b]1995 data; [c]1994 data; [d]1993 data
Source: derived from Anderson and Poullier (1999: 183), based on OECD (1998)

lower than those of specialists. There is widespread concern that the United States is not producing enough GPs and other primary care providers. Non-physician providers, such as nurse practitioners and physician assistants, can perform many of the services which doctors now perform.

High incomes are a product of the pricing arrangements, which have limited flexibility to adjust prices downwards. Traditionally, pricing was established by making price comparisons in relation to what others charge, and insurance programmes such as Medicare calculate payments on the basis of prevailing rates. Medicare's introduction of the resource based relative value scale (RBRVS) and volume performance standards has changed these practices. Spending levels increased by 12.1 per cent between 1980 and 1989, but only by 4.8 per cent between 1989 and 1993 (White 1995: 84). However, there are concerns that unless other purchasers are prepared to pay less (Medicare's fees are substantially lower than the average private fee) some providers will refuse to care for Medicare patients.

Proposals for reform

In the US system, providers compete for patients on the strength of the services they offer. Patients, with the exception of those in HMOs and PPOs, have direct access to primary care physicians, to most specialists and to most hospitals. Providers take considerable measures to protect themselves against accusations of medical malpractice. In addition to taking out insurance, they also tend to provide diagnostic testing and care which is described as 'defensive medicine'.

In response to the escalating costs and inequities in the system, President Clinton made health care reform a top policy priority, and proposals were developed to introduce universal coverage by 1998. Purchasing was to be achieved through regional health alliances, corporate alliances (for firms with more than 5000 workers), and through Medicare, for those not in the workforce. Alliances would offer individuals one of three types of health plan: HMOs, PPOs or fee-for-service arrangements. Each would be responsible for: charging a community rate; accepting anyone who wanted to enrol; guaranteeing renewal; and eliminating pre-existing condition exclusions (Cutler 1994: 22).

Following intense lobbying by the medical profession, insurance industry and others, the reforms were rejected. Despite this, some aspects of what was proposed are being implemented to a degree. The US health system is undergoing change as it attempts to contain costs and redress inequities. There is a move towards managed care, more comprehensive disease management and strategies which keep people healthy. The competitive nature of managed care arrangements has elevated quality of care and health care outcomes as criteria for individuals and companies wishing to join particular HMOs and PPOs.

States are taking the public policy lead in reforming health care, as illustrated by changes in the states of Oregon, Hawaii and Florida. Oregon introduced a three-part programme, its section 1115 Medicaid demonstration project under the Oregon Health Plan. Medicaid eligibility has been expanded and a system devised for determining what should be funded. This was done by ranking conditions and treatments to prioritize care, based on a core list. This list is now commonly referred to as the basic benefits package. The funding of medical procedures by the Medicaid budget is based on the ranking of the condition. In the first year, only mothers and children who qualified for Aid to Families with Dependent Children (AFDC) were covered. The Oregon plan was implemented on 1 January 1995 and has proved to be quite successful in maintaining costs while at the same time extending the coverage of Medicaid in the state (Burton 1996).

Since 1974, Hawaii has had compulsory employer-subsidized insurance for employees who work 20 or more hours per week, resulting in near-universal coverage of the working population though not extending to dependants. Since 1990, Hawaii has offered the State Health Insurance Program (SHIP) to low-income people. Together with Medicaid, these programmes allow Hawaii to obtain 93 per cent health insurance cover for those under 65 years of age. In August 1994, the state combined SHIP, AFDC and general assistance programmes into one managed care programme administered by the Hawaii Department of Human Services. The programme has reduced wastage and includes capitation measures, a strong emphasis on communication, central coordination of services and an assessment of service delivery (Thorne *et al.* 1995).

Florida passed legislation aimed at encouraging employers to voluntarily improve cover. Instigated in 1993, Community Health Purchasing Agreements help small companies to contract for health insurance coverage. Small businesses tend to fail more often, offer less cushioning for financial losses, and leave insurers less time to build up financial reserves. The programme is a means of pooling the fiscal risk to allow affordable premiums for businesses with fewer staff (Cox 1998).

Until 1998 there was dramatic growth of managed care organizations entering the Medicare market as a profit-making strategy. However, the Balanced Budget Act 1997 changed this trend, as inflation-related increases in Medicare risk plans for 1999 were capped at 2 per cent (Bell 1998a), in contrast to the 8.3 per cent increase that HMOs were seeking for 1999. Increased general costs and the spiralling cost of prescription drugs pushed many managed care organizations into deficit, resulting in some of them notifying the Health Care Financing Administration of plans to withdraw from Medicare and Medicaid markets (Bell 1998b; Jacob 1998; Hudson *et al.* 1999).

System impacts

Efficiency

The US system exhibits sources of inefficiency and significant problems of market failure. These problems include cost-unconscious demand, biased risk selection as an important source of profit, market segmentation minimizing price competition, lack of information, limited choice and perverse public subsidies (Enthoven 1993: 11). State employee health plans are among the largest group purchasers of health insurance. It has been found that states that contributed a more generous share of premiums (80–100 per cent) and covered benefits more comprehensively, achieved fewer efficiency gains than those exposing families to relatively high premium shares (Schoen *et al.*, in Ginzberg 1994: 220). Third-party payers reduce incentives in the system to restrain demand. 'The fragmented US structure gives providers incentives to deliver additional services and to bill for higher levels of service so as to increase revenues' (OECD 1994: 326).

System features thwart efforts to improve allocative and technical efficiency. The nature of the tax-subsidized insurance industry means that some people obtain more insurance cover and use more health care than they would if they were paying for it out-of-pocket. Insurance coverage arrangements encourage the delivery of care which is not cost-effective (Termeer and Raines 1994: 56). The system is characterized by excess capacity of hospital resources, overproduction of procedure-oriented care, an oversupply of highly paid specialists, inflated premium prices, high administrative costs, large numbers of people with excess insurance cover, and a large number of uninsured persons. All this has contributed to making the US health care system the most costly in the industrialized world.

Evidence suggests that between 17 and 30 per cent of frequently performed surgical and diagnostic procedures are inappropriate (Aday *et al.* 1993). Some of the overused practices include 400,000 unnecessary Caesarean sections each year, MRI scans, and about 30 per cent of acute care services. At the same time there is an underutilization of primary care and preventative services. There is low use of inexpensive medications such as aspirin and beta blocker drugs for heart-related care, and only one-third of asthmatic patients receive inhaled steroid medications to prevent disability and complications (Egger, 1999: 13). Apart from Medicaid, there is a lack of integration between long-term and acute care services. There has been a steady increase in the number of group practices relative to solo practices since 1970, and larger practices have fostered efficiency by enjoying economies of scale.

Insurers are attempting to address the problem of moral hazard through co-insurance and innovations in managed care (NERA 1993: 2). Inefficiency arises from the behaviour of the uninsured, who tend to present at emergency rooms, where they often get expensive and inappropriate forms of treatment. These costs are then indirectly built into the insurance premiums of the paying customer. It has been estimated that the cost of coverage for the uninsured is about US$22 billion a year (Gold 1993: 24).

There is excess capacity in the hospital system: each day over 35 per cent of acute hospital beds are empty (Go 1994: 18). Excess capacity has come about partly because the system has been funded on a cost-plus basis. In 1992, Medicare changed its capital reimbursement rules, though effectiveness is reduced by several loopholes that remain.

There are no federal controls on the proliferation of expensive medical technology. The industry is subsidized federally, and only limited state regulations exist. Americans have come to expect health technology to be available to them, and technology is the cornerstone of competition between providers. Often, new technologies spread before evaluative studies have been completed.

Efficiency gains have been made by improving access to second opinions, profile analysis of provider utilization and practice patterns, and screening of claims prior to payment. To improve efficiency and curb costs, private insurers have introduced some **gatekeeping** measures in hospital care and specialist services and placed greater emphasis on outpatient care, particularly following surgery. In the 1980s, Medicare introduced a prospective payment system for hospitals. This has been successful at improving efficiency. In particular the average number of days in a hospital stay dropped dramatically when hospitals were paid on a per case rather than per diem basis (Moon 1994; Anderson and Poullier 1999). HMOs, in particular, have targeted cost-saving measures in the funding of services.

A growing number of third-party payers have also shifted from retrospective to prospective payment arrangements with providers, though prospective payment systems can increase costs. Since payments are based on diagnosis, it is in the interest of both hospitals and physicians to admit patients. DRG-based Medicare funding has promoted efficiency for in-patient services. However, a problem known as 'bracket' or 'DRG creep' can lead to an increase in the number of people receiving a particular well-paid diagnosis, resulting in a higher reimbursement rate to the hospital. It is anticipated that further attempts will be made to reduce Medicare expenditure, although an initial attempt by federal authorities to raise Medicare eligibility from 65 to 67 years of age failed.

Medicare has low administrative overheads, accounting for less than 3 per cent of spending, compared with about 10 per cent for large private health insurance companies and as much as 40 per cent in a small group market (Moon 1994: 174). The average administrative cost is usually quoted as 25 per cent. Parts of the high costs are incurred on advertising and competing for patients. Administrative inefficiency is also encouraged by the fragmented nature of the system. 'Patient care is difficult to co-ordinate and manage effectively when many physicians, hospitals, and other providers are solo operators who function autonomously' (Go 1994: 18). Each of these providers often has to bill the purchaser separately for a particular contribution to care. This can mean multiple billing for a hospital admission. The development of HMOs and PPOs is addressing this inefficiency. The large-scale purchaser–provider mergers that have taken place should help to reduce administrative costs by avoiding the duplication of administrative functions.

While it is common to compare the performance of different countries in terms of levels of spending and measures of health status, there is limited analysis of system performance in terms of efficiency. One study of interest, however, examines technical efficiency across three countries – Germany, the UK and the United States. The analysis shows that, while service delivery in the

United States is sometimes more efficient than in the other countries, higher prices and administrative costs (rather than higher outputs and productivity) explain the higher spending levels in that country (Baily and Garber 1997).

Cost containment

A prime focus for health policy has been on cost containment. In the Clinton reforms this was to be achieved by a cap on premiums in the alliances. Other strategies include standardized benefits, improved price and quality information, incentives for people to join less expensive plans, and the introduction of gatekeepers and managed care arrangements to reduce access to specialists and to hospital services. Increased entrepreneurialism in the insurance industry has compelled firms to minimize costs so as to meet the expectations of investment-owned purchasing and providing organizations (Tuohy 1999: 125).

The US health system remains the most expensive among the industrialized nations. Each resident in the United States has US$3925 per capita spent on health, against the OECD average of US$1728 (Anderson and Poullier 1999). Although total health care spending has remained a major issue for the reform of the system, the emphasis has moved towards reviewing the system of delivery to promote cost-efficiency (Davis 1999). The integration of purchasers and providers through managed care arrangements has been the key strategy to reduce wastage within the system. However, few employers deal with health outcomes or the quality of care provided; curbing costs remains the primary objective for employers who provide insurance (Shalala and Reinhardt 1999). Cost-cutting measures in the 1990s have included curbing tests, surgery, referrals to specialists and hospital stays considered unnecessary, paying lower fees, promoting prevention and seeking out efficiencies wherever possible. In regions where HMOs have begun to compete for business, evidence shows that they have stabilizing health care expenditure (Eckholm 1994: 34). Based on previous evidence, however, successful cost containment is likely to be short-lived (Morgello 1993).

While savings have resulted from a dramatic reduction length of stays in hospitals, there has been pressure on pharmaceutical expenditure (Tuohy 1999). The United States experienced a 23 per cent increase in prescription drug spending between 1992 and 1996, related to the growth of managed care plans: these plans tend to use prescription drugs in disease management schemes in the community.

Intensive use of technology and high rates of physician specialization have constrained efforts to achieve cost savings. Physician incomes in the United States actually increased above the inflation rate between 1960 and 1996, with an average wage of US$199,000 in 1996, a level well above any other OECD country (Anderson and Poullier 1999: 187).

Equity

Inequities arise from a number of sources. Low-income people cannot afford the insurance premiums, and either do not insure or accept minimal coverage. The least healthy people pay the highest premiums; the sickest are often the poorest. Even programmes aimed at low-income populations exclude many. The financial cut-off points are often well below the poverty line (some reports suggest 30 per cent below), and criteria for cover discriminate against young, single people. However, the federal government does provide an income subsidy in such situations. People with previous health problems cannot afford to pay the actuarially adjusted rates. Reliance on consumer choice and competition has increased inequities in the system as programmes have been designed to select risk. Even legislated risk-pooled insurance in many states is beyond the reach of many, and requires substantial state subsidies. There are incentives for HMOs to select only low-risk patients into their schemes.

The distribution of spending is very uneven across the population. National data on the concentration of health expenditures reveal that the sickest 1 per cent of the population accounts for 30 per cent of all expenses, while the sickest 10 per cent accounts for a 72 per cent share. Meanwhile the healthiest half of the population accounts for only 3 per cent of total expenses (Schoen *et al.*, in Ginzberg 1994: 216).

The size and type of the workplace influences whether an employee is likely to obtain insurance through their job. Those on higher earnings in larger firms are much more likely to receive health insurance through the workplace than those in small organizations on low salaries. The type of business also affects the availability and cost of insurance. There has been blacklisting of entire industries, especially for insurance sold to small and medium-sized firms. Insurance for many is thus becoming harder to obtain (Weiner 1994: 3).

There is a geographical maldistribution of providers between rural and urban settings and richer and poorer states. The trend towards market consolidation in health care insurance and pur-chaser–provider mergers is likely to focus attention more on profit-ability and less on access. There is concern that these large organizations will show little regard for access, quality of care and social equity (Weil 1996). Severe inequities arise in continuity of care, and those without private insurance receive fewer and less coordinated services (OECD 1994).

Choice

Traditionally, consumers in the United States could choose their purchasers and providers; however, this is rapidly changing with the growth of HMOs and PPOs. A series of federal waivers have allowed states to move those eligible for Medicaid into managed care (Shalala and Reinhardt 1999). There is growing consumer dis-satisfaction at the lack of flexibility and choice within managed care agreements. Critics of managed care arrangements fear its impact on patient quality and there are concerns that physician frustration may derail the cost savings achieved in the mid-1990s (Kovach 1998). Doctors have had to relinquish control over their decisions and incomes to managed care organizations. For example, during 1993–94, the share of managed care contracts among doctors work-ing in group practices jumped from 56 per cent to 89 per cent (Eck-holm 1994). Partnerships also developed between providers and purchasers (physician–hospital organizations called PHOs), where, for a set fee, a hospital agreed to provide all health care for an employee (Morgello 1993).

Consumers and medical personnel are also objecting to the incon-venience associated with increased use of primary care doctors as gatekeepers to specialist treatment. This is now being felt in US health care as a backlash to managed care service delivery (Kovach 1998; Blendon *et al.* 1999). Choice still exists for those who can afford it; however, for the majority, the implementation of managed care arrangements and mergers of health insurance companies have limited the choice of insurance policies at affordable prices.

Some critics suggest that choice is illusionary, since the options are often too complex for the individual. On the other hand, the range of choice available has also posed problems, as the relatively healthy, well-informed segment of the population has learned to switch in and out of plans based on their expected medical care needs. Plans have also used 'tactical and subtle benefit differences to improve their risk mix'. This has led to plans being forced to expand or contract their operations very suddenly (Schoen *et al.*, in Ginzberg 1994: 218).

Conclusion

The greater the costs of health care cover, the more difficult it becomes to finance and maintain insurance coverage. The reforms attempted by President Clinton in 1994 tried to deal with problems of health externalities by introducing universal coverage, but the proposals failed to gain the required level of political support.

A major issue facing the future of the US health care industry is the decrease in take-up rates of private insurance among the employed population. Rising costs in the system have been addressed by regulation from within the industry and by managed care arrangements. Key issues are the relationship between premium costs and coverage levels, and the assignment of responsibility to subsidize the uninsured between the state and current policyholders.

The continued plurality of the health sector and the presence of a large uninsured population dominate the health policy debate. The majority of purchasers have adopted managed care in an effort to improve efficiencies, which has led to a major reorganization in the provision of health care. It has also placed greater accountability on clinical delivery systems, although the structural overhaul of clinical organizations is lagging behind. The trend towards large health networks and managed care plans is proving beneficial in cost-containment terms, but is creating pressures for regulatory changes and raising concerns about the erosion of consumer choice.

CANADA

Canada is a federation consisting of ten provinces and two northern territories. Tensions between the English-speaking majority of Canadians and those from the French-speaking province of Quebec have encouraged the decentralization of health policy-making to the provincial level. This is underpinned by the 1867 Constitution Act which assigns jurisdiction to the provinces over health care institutions' professional licensure.

Public and private roles

Canada's health system includes elements of both public and private financing, purchasing and provision of health care. The funding and purchasing arrangements are shared across different levels of government and competing private insurers. A single public purchaser exists and supplementary insurance is provided by competing private insurers. The Canadian system is unusual in terms of the interface between public and private funding systems. The legislative and regulatory framework does not permit private (for-profit) insurance for any hospital and medical services which are classified as 'medically necessary'. This distinguishes it from many other systems in which individuals use private insurance to get quicker access to core services. At the same time, the definition of core services has gaps, for example in areas like pharmaceuticals. This can lead to substantial out-of-pocket expenses for those without private insurance cover.

Medicare, Canada's universal, comprehensive and mandatory hospital and medical insurance scheme, funds about 75 per cent of the costs of care, which is delivered at the point of service with no co-payments. Funding is via a national graduated progressive tax system, though, in British Columbia and Alberta only, some funding is obtained from health insurance premiums. Provincial payroll and sales taxes may also be utilized for financing health care.

There are substantial economic disparities among provinces, and therefore any effort to operate a universal national system through provincial funding schemes would result in major discrepancies in the quality and availability of services. The Canadian response has been to utilize the concept of fiscal federalism as a vehicle for substantial transfers of resources from the richer provinces (such as Ontario, British Columbia and Alberta) to the rest of the country. Various cost-sharing programmes exist in the areas of hospital and medical insurance. The Canada Health Act 1984 gave provinces full federal funding if their health systems complied with five national standards: (1) universality, (2) accessibility, (3) comprehensiveness, (4) portability, and (5) public administration, the last including a non-profit status (Department of National Health and Welfare 1992a).

The Medicare system was developed as a compromise between the public's wish to have universal medical coverage, and limitations arising from constitutional and political difficulties. Medicare is a set of parallel provincial insurance schemes, each of which controls the organization and payment of health care institutions and providers.

In order to limit federal expenditure, each province is given a federal block grant, which is called Established Programme Financing (EPF), and then administers its own provincial health plan (Department of National Health and Welfare 1992b). Provincial authorities, following federal guidelines decide how much money will be spent on health, whether to insure services beyond those of the national policy, and how to finance the province's share of the costs. The system's reliance on general taxation for funding means that there is no direct link between tax or premium payment and health services received, reflecting the principles of equity and ability to pay. The social insurance scheme covers necessary hospital costs and doctors' fees for 100 per cent of the population. Individuals receiving these subsidized services pay nothing at the point of use. The system allows risks to be pooled across the population and the scheme serves to redistribute resources from low to high risk.

Health care costs for employees are organized by provincial workers' compensation boards, which are funded by employer contributions and cover employees injured at work. Private insurance is also available and covers other services such as dental care, optical care, prescription drugs, and semi-private and private hospital rooms. Around 80 per cent of the population has this type of additional insurance, most of which is financed by employers. The largest item of expenditure in these supplementary plans is prescription drugs, which account for almost three-quarters of all employer-financed supplementary benefits. Growth in pharmaceutical costs has been substantial and various strategies, including reference-based pricing and generic substitution, have been used to promote more effective and efficient resource use. Many provincial systems provide benefits to particular groups to assist with these costs, while the province of Saskatchewan has introduced a universal tax-supported drug plan.

As of 1996 the share of private sector spending was 30 per cent. Between the mid-1970s and 1996 the average level of federal spending on health declined from 42 per cent to 20 per cent and per capita entitlements were frozen for two years in 1990. Growth in health expenditures was 42 per cent for all provinces in the late 1990s, while federal transfers for this period remained constant. Each of Canada's provinces spends about one-third of its yearly budget on health care. Health care expenditures as a percentage of GDP were 8.5 per cent in the mid-1980s and 9.9 per cent by 1991 (Rathwell

1994), but dropped to 9.0 per cent by 1997. Rising costs, coupled with several economic pressures, have put the Canadian health system under considerable strain. Financial deficits at the federal level resulted in cutbacks to expenditure and the election of provincial governments committed to fiscal restraint. Substantial cuts to public funding were imposed at both the federal and provincial levels over a period of several years.

In 1994, residents of Ontario paid the most for private health care (C\$790 per person), while those in Newfoundland contributed the least (C\$538 per person) (Rafuse 1996). There are now pressures on the system to allow greater private funding, and to clarify the nature and circumstances under which services are to be subsidized. Creating a workable definition of core versus non-core services has proved difficult, in part because cost-effectiveness in health is often person-specific (Deber and Baranek 1998).

Canada's system embraces a holistic approach to health which includes physical, social and psychological factors, as well as lifestyle characteristics. The system has strong support from its citizens and embraces the concept of universalism. Yet some provincial reform documents are signalling a shift from community to individual responsibility and the need for greater cost containment as part of strategies for managing budgetary pressures (Iannantuono and Eyles 1997).

Each provincial government acts as a monopsony buyer of necessary medical services, with patients taking no direct part in the reimbursement of hospital and physician services. Capital expenditure for hospitals and long-term care facilities is publicly financed, though ownership and service delivery may reside with non-profit societies. There are also regional and municipal contributions and some private capital for establishments operating in the area of long-term care. Health services are provided by private practitioners, paid on a fee-for-service basis, non-profit voluntary organizations that are funded by grants from the Ministry of Health, and programmes delivered by government ministries. Benefits and services to target populations receive higher subsidies, which vary across the provinces (Lovelace and Sedgwick 1996).

The majority of GPs operate independent practices, and submit their claims for payment to the provincial health insurance plans. GPs are reimbursed through a schedule of fixed rates set by the provincial medical association. Rates are constrained by the total percentage increase in the fee base, as negotiated between the medical association and the government. It is illegal for doctors to impose charges in excess of fees agreed by provincial insurance plans. This phenomenon, known as extra-billing, occurred throughout the 1970s and early 1980s, and caused access problems. To combat this trend, the Canada Health Act 1984 introduced dollar-for-dollar deductions for any province which allowed extra billing or user charges, and by 1987, extra billing and user charges were eliminated from the system.

The 1993 distribution of health expenditures by category was: hospitals 38 per cent, physicians 15 per cent, drugs 15 per cent, other institutions 10 per cent, other professionals 6 per cent, other expenditures 12 per cent, and capital 4 per cent (Leatt and Williams 1997). Physicians play a central role, acting as primary providers of medical services, gatekeepers to the system, resource allocators and patient advocates.

Delivery of services is conducted mainly by the private sector: the majority of hospitals are private, non-profit institutions, while physicians are generally self-employed and are paid on a fee-for-service basis. The system does allow, however, privately funded services to exist in parallel. Most jurisdictions give physicians the choice of practising either wholly within or wholly outside the publicly funded system. Doctors may opt out and serve a patient population willing to pay the entire cost of services. Patients have free choice of primary care physician, who acts as gatekeeper and controls referrals to specialists and hospitals.

Regulatory bodies cover each health profession and have responsibilities for establishing and monitoring standards. The bodies are organized on a provincial basis and vary in terms of their interest in quality assurance and accountability. Some provinces have legislation governing health professionals which requires providers to develop a quality assurance programme, though responsibility for implementing the legislation rests with hospitals. A national system exists for voluntary hospital and long-term care accreditation. Traditionally, physicians have enjoyed considerable economic and clinical freedoms. While changes are occurring, voluntarism prevails with regard to practice guidelines, quality assurance programmes for continuing education and recertification (Leatt and Williams 1997).

Physicians are becoming more active in health management and policy issues and there is growing interest in seeking some accommodation with the government. In Ontario, the Joint Committee on Physician Services has been established with the Ministry of Health to allow the profession greater input to policy matters.

Proposals for reform

The Canadian system ranks as one of the more expensive systems in the world. Although the main thrust of the Canadian reforms of the late 1980s and 1990s was efficiency, many strategies placed their focus on cost containment, with a view to making improvements in technical efficiency. Hospital costs were contained through global prospective budgets and control over the use of high-cost technologies. Many reviews of the health system have suggested the need for greater decentralization of resource allocation and service delivery. Problems of service coordination exist, particularly at the primary care level. The separation of physician and pharmaceutical reimbursement systems limits the potential for integrated primary care funding and delivery. Ontario has established the Comprehensive Health Organization which operates very much like an American health maintenance organization (Naylor 1992), though there has been limited attention given to primary care strategies and capitation-based funding approaches.

The 1990s saw considerable strain placed upon the health system arising from the federal government's progressive withdrawal of funding. In the mid-1990s, the federal Liberal government rolled a number of social transfers into the Canada Health and Social Transfer (CHST) fund with a view to establishing a stable federal floor to funding for the Canada Health Acts. At the same time, provincial governments were given more discretion to modify the instruments and systems surrounding health care organization and delivery. This resulted in many provincial governments increasing their authority over the governance of hospitals. In February 1999, in the midst of growing public concern, the government announced plans for a phased-in restoration of federal transfers for health to approximately their nominal pre-CHST level. While a small loosening of fiscal constraints may ease the pressures on the system, it will not reduce the need to find new strategies to improve the efficiency of the system.

Some key issues for the policy agenda are likely to surround the question of the funding of pharmaceuticals on a more equitable basis, measures to improve service coordination and to shift care from institutional settings to community and home-based settings. Policy-makers are giving attention to the establishment of a national accountability framework, including the possibility of a national report card which would allow for the establishment of best practice and systems for comparing provincial policies and performance (Tuohy 1999: 17).

The spending cuts of the late 1990s have challenged the traditional role in the system of the federal government. Financial pressures at the federal and state levels raised issues of targeting, rationing or limiting the government's coverage of care. Unmet demand is creating support for extending the role of private institutions and private clinics. Private clinics are now developing which provide 'necessary' hospital services, the costs of which are being financed through the private insurance system. Even the restrictions against user charges have been challenged as Quebec has introduced a small user charge for non-urgent outpatient treatment in public hospitals.

There is support for the private sector among some groups, including parts of the medical profession. Support is growing for greater competition among private and public insurers and for proposals which extend the role of private insurance in funding both basic and supplementary care. One proposal from the Fraser Institute suggests that individuals should each receive a medical premium account which is funded by the government but apportioned by the patient. Regional purchasers would be established with exclusive power to purchase health services for patients in their regions. The proposal provides for individuals to opt out of the public system and seek health care from the private sector (Rafuse 1996).

Rather than pursuing a purchaser–provider split, the Canadian health care system has created horizontally integrated organizations at regional and local levels. Emphasis has been placed on collaboration rather than competition, maintaining strong community involvement, coupled with needs assessment and improved approaches to resource allocation.

System impacts

Efficiency

Because health services are not directly paid for when they are delivered, there is a tendency for users to overconsume health services and to demand care whose marginal cost may exceed the marginal benefits. Critics of the system claim that users' expectations of free care causes the system to overprovide routine medical services for the majority of the population. This leads to allocative inefficiency as attention is given to first-round care for sniffles and splinters, rather than directing resources to the minority with specialized needs, so better outcomes can be achieved. The tendency for users to demand care which may not be efficient is mirrored by the fee-for-service payments systems which give medical providers some strong financial incentives to supply extra services.

There is evidence to support the hypothesis that physician-induced demand exists. Physicians have incentives to overservice, particularly since patients judge doctors on the quality of their care, and not price. Physicians' incomes under this system are directly determined by how many medical services they provide each day, with the result that doctors are encouraged to provide unnecessary services that cost billions of tax dollars each year. Fee-for-service gives physicians incentives to treat patients with remedies, especially prescription drugs, which require return visits for check-ups and prescription renewals (York 1992).

Some incentives on individual physicians are offset by contracts with professional associations governing payments to physicians. The government has been working to establish cost-containment strategies which make doctors more conscious about overall levels of servicing, for example by the use of contracts which specify both prices per unit of service and volumes. Medicare also imposes a maximum payment that can be claimed by a physician.

Debate surrounds the efficiency of prospective global budgeting for hospitals. Some suggest that global budgets encourage efficiency and prioritizing, and many provinces have incorporated savings-retention programmes to maintain strong incentives (Neuschler 1990). However, experience of global budgeting for hospitals indicates that allocative efficiency is not being realized: a health advisory committee in Ontario concluded that global budgeting: '(1) discouraged bottom-up responsibility for controlling costs and encouraged a growth mentality; (2) failed to address inequities in hospital budgets; and (3) focused on management efficiency rather than health outcomes' (Graig 1991: 461). Global budgeting can provide incentives for hospitals to cut expenditures too far and to stretch dollars by filling acute-care beds with low-cost, long-term patients, whose daily medical requirements are well below average. Health care providers estimate that such 'bed-blockers' occupy around 15 per cent of acute-care beds (Graig 1991).

Canada has lower health sector employment levels than Australia and the United States, and there is a tendency to use well educated and well paid personnel. The highly unionized health care labour market limits opportunities for substituting less costly personnel to perform services under supervision (Stoddart and Barer 1992). A similar concern arises, especially in urban areas, from the involvement of specialists in providing primary care. Operational expenses and capital spending are separated in hospital budgeting. Arrangements for the funding of capital acquisitions vary across provinces, but common features include prior approval by the provincial minister of health based on needs assessment and the compulsory participation of municipal governments and/or privately raised funds (10–40 per cent). Since the authority to approve an expansion rests with the agency that will have to cover ongoing operating costs, approval is not given lightly. Governments have some control over the diffusion of technology, as hospitals must seek grants from the Ministry of Health for high-technology equipment. However, governments have minimal control over low start-up cost, high-volume procedures. Provincial governments lack adequate accountability systems and the media play a prominent role in holding provincial government purchasers to account for access and technology-related problems. However, provincial governments are constrained in their ability to call hospitals to account because of their limited authority over the use of hospital resources. Health ministries do not monitor expenditures on a case-by-case basis, and have limited influence over the inefficient use of acute-care hospitals. As budgets are not based on individual patient costs, hospitals have little incentive to develop detailed information systems (Graig 1991).

Having a single public agency administer health insurance in each province concentrates financial responsibility with a single payer. This promotes efficient administration, particularly compared with the US system where numerous private companies and public agencies administer insurance programmes. The single-payer system simplifies the process of paying claims. Each province issues a health plan charge card to each resident, and providers submit the card number with the claim for full reimbursement from the provincial government. Canada's universal coverage means that there are no costs associated with determining eligibility. Insurance system administration does not involve such costs as marketing expenses, estimating risk to set differential premiums, deciding who to cover, approving hospital admissions, or allocating shareholder profits (Graig 1991).

Administration costs for Canada are low, representing approximately 2 per cent of total health costs (Bennett and Adams 1993). From the providers' point of view, the simple claims procedures are administratively efficient, and Canadian physicians are not involved in insurance record-keeping, direct billing of patients, or the collection of bad debts. Hospitals tend to have virtually no billing departments, and minimal accounting structures to assign costs and charges to patients and physicians. However, some academics have challenged the administrative efficiency of public insurance schemes, suggesting that accounting measures give misleading and partial estimates of the full overhead costs of delivering insured medical services. While public insurers generate lower observable direct accounting costs, there are much higher hidden costs. While private insurers must induce voluntary participation, governments are able to coerce people to pay taxes, to accept prices and restrictions on services, and to bear risk (Danzon 1992: 22).

Cost containment

The Canadian system evolved from a US-style health care system and has made progress in its efforts to contain costs, as measured in relation to real health expenditures per capita or health care's share of GNP. Nor is performance just a by-product of the growth rate of GNP (Marmor 1993). The dominant position of public insurers is the key weapon which underpins strategies for cost containment and efficiency. Buyers, through their political representatives, bargain with providers over price and quantity of care, and control overall system costs in a way that individual patients cannot (Evans 1987). Hospitals' cost-efficient measures include bulk purchasing of drugs and other items, contracting-out of laundry and meal services, merging departments with similar or complementary functions, and shifting services to outpatient facilities.

The fee-for-service payment system gives physicians an incentive to extend service levels. Some provinces have attempted to introduce co-payments for services not seen as medically necessary (OECD 1994). Financial pressure in recent times has acted to lower the level of extended benefits by various means, including 'de-insuring' benefits not deemed medically necessary, more restrictive definitions of specific groups entitled to benefits, and greater caution in extending entitlement to new services and therapies.

Reforms have occurred in the areas of publicly funded home care and community services, and several provinces have established a single point of entry for long-term care in the 1980s. This operates on the principle that necessary care will be provided at the least costly level, and non-institutional services will be used as the first stage of long-term care (OECD 1994). For example, Canada traditionally had a high proportion of its elderly population in long-term care institutions; since the 1980s there have been shifts towards services which assist people to remain in their homes, such as emergency response teams, home nursing and support, respite care, meals on wheels, visiting services and adult day programmes. Following a long series of reviews and proposals for reform, the government introduced a purchaser–provider split in the area of long-term care, leaving the government largely in the role of purchasing services from a capped budget from competing for-profit and not-for-profit providers.

Equity

Canada's social insurance system promotes equity by providing a universal minimum standard of care. The portability principle provides similar benefits to individuals who require services while in another province. The Canada Health Act 1984 does not require, however, that the level of services provided in a given province be comparable to that of insured persons in other Canadian jurisdictions (Boothe and Johnston 1993: 7). Reciprocal medical claim arrangements apply among the provinces (OECD 1994).

The discretion held by provinces produces considerable variation in the range of extended benefits on offer. The differences include both eligibility provisions and levels of coverage offered in areas like drugs and dental benefits. Payments between provinces for high-cost procedures and outpatients are set at the inter-provincial level and apply nationwide. Other hospital services are billed at per diem rates negotiated between provinces. National standards have been seen as important for the Canadians, and there have been occasions where federal funding has been withheld to force compliance with the Canada Health Act (Boothe and Johnston 1993: 2). Reduced federal funding has limited the power of the federal government to enforce national standards. Within provincial systems, greater emphasis has been given to allocating funding on the basis of some assessment of need, using measures of population adjusted for other dimensions including age, sex and, in some cases, health status. For example, in British Columbia the Ministry of Health entered into block contracts with selected hospitals and funds activities such as cardiac surgery and angioplasty (Lovelace and Sedgwick 1996).

As private insurance companies are not allowed to provide cover for medical services already insured by social insurance schemes, the system aims to prevent a two-tiered structure from emerging. The Canadian system embodies redistributional elements in a way that private insurance cannot. Individuals' contributions to the funding of health care are detached from their expected risk and from receipt of care, so that contributions are on an ability-to-pay basis and wealth is redistributed from low-risk to high-risk individuals. Provinces which charge premiums as a source of financing care offer premium assistance for those on low incomes in order to protect their income sufficiency (Department of National Health and Welfare 1992b).

Despite the emphasis on universal access to health services, problems have developed and have manifested themselves in waiting lists and rationing. There are no clear-cut criteria for deciding rationing priorities, which leads to inequities among patients with different conditions. The system's commitment to provide routine treatment to the majority of the population may also hinder vertical equity, by diverting resources away from the minority with specialized needs. Long waiting lists have encouraged some individuals to seek private treatment in the United States. A 1996 estimate suggested that over C$1 billion each year was spent by wealthy Canadians to access care in the United States; a level which represents a loss of 10,000 Canadian jobs (Dirnfeld 1996).

The system faces long-standing difficulties in distributing care appropriately across different regions. Attempts to alter the rewards to doctors have met opposition from professional groups. Greater reliance on provincial funding will serve to increase the differences in care across provinces. The fiscal problems of the 1990s have led to the establishment of private clinics, funded by private insurance, providing similar services to those covered by public insurance.

Choice

Canadians have free choice of general practitioners who control referrals to specialists and hospital admissions. However, regulations governing the coverage of private insurance limit opportunities for individuals to supplement their coverage through the universal system. This is unlike the practice in many other countries, where faster access to elective surgery may be funded through private insurance.

In recent years the Canadian health system has made efforts to decentralize decision-making and to amalgamate management and service delivery systems to regional structures. The devolution is inspired by a desire to facilitate consumer choice, while the amalgamation is aimed at creating management efficiencies via a more integrated system of care.

Conclusion

Of the various policy goals, equity has played an important role relative to efficiency. Increasingly, however, budgetary pressures have made cost containment the primary objective, with implications for differences in access across provinces. The direct funding of pharmaceuticals, hospitals and doctor fees limits the potential for decentralized competitive mechanisms to improve allocative and technical efficiency. While consultative mechanisms exist, the overall system provides limited choice for service users.

While Canadians may have a choice of doctor, the health system is doctor-focused and resource decisions remain in the hands of physicians. The failure of doctors to contain costs is likely to result in a growing role for managers in influencing practice, which in turn will increase tensions between managers and physicians.

Concerns about cost containment have also made the government reluctant to fund new technological developments. Recent cuts in funding to the provinces have placed the basic underpinning of the Canada Health Act at risk. While some of the funding cuts were reversed, growing reliance on provincial spending is increasing provincial variation in levels of services.

The Canadian system has shown how cost containment and equity can be fostered when the government acts as a monopsony insurer. Contracts with providers which include an element of risk-sharing have been successful in exerting leverage on service utilization and system costs.

AUSTRALIA

Australia has a population of 18 million, and levels are projected to reach over 21 million by 2011 (AIHW 1996). The indigenous people, the Aboriginal and Torres Strait Islanders, constitute 1.7 per cent of the population. The country is highly urbanized and 80 per cent of the population lives in coastal cities, while the interior of the country remains largely unpopulated.

Australia is a federal state, divided into six states and two terri-tories, with a federal bicameral parliament. With the exception of Queensland, the states have bicameral parliaments, with more than nine hundred local bodies beneath the state parliaments. Govern-ment policies on health involve many units of government operat-ing at the federal, state and local levels. This results in regional and local variations in the funding, purchasing and delivery arrange-ments and in priorities across policy goals.

Public and private roles

The Commonwealth maintains responsibility for health policy, the funding of health care services, health research and promotion. A Commonwealth Department of Health was not established until 1921 and for many years its main responsibilities were quarantine and the health needs of veterans. An amendment of the Consti-tution in 1946 gave the Commonwealth powers to make laws about pharmaceuticals, sickness and hospital benefits, and medical and dental services. These powers and the provision of specific-purpose grants to states have enabled the Commonwealth to expand its role in the health system.

State and territory health authorities are responsible for hospital services, mental health programmes, dental health services, home and community care, child, adolescent and family health services, women's health programmes, rehabilitation systems and regu-lation, inspection, licensing and monitoring of premises, institutions and personnel. The Commonwealth government exerts control over states through the use of funding mechanisms. Australians who wish to do so can obtain services from a large private sector.

Local governments participate in the areas of environmental control and preventative services. State governments take responsi-bility for budgeting and finance, labour relations, major capital investment, and the majority of public acute-care hospitals. Strong community-based networks have been integrated into the public system. These networks have reduced per capita hospital stays by allowing earlier discharge for medical patients and facilitating treatment of geriatric and mental health patients in the community rather than in hospitals (Peabody *et al.* 1996).

Governments have assumed an important role in the promotion of general health, the provision of resources to measure health stan-dards, evaluation of health services, and the promotion of disease management. Focus has been directed towards control of alcohol and drug abuse, dental health, and controlling the spread of AIDS (AIHW 1998). Successful interventions in the area of population health can be traced to innovative partnerships between public and non-governmental groups.

Structures surrounding various Commonwealth, state and territory health authorities have experienced frequent change, involving reorganization, amalgamations and the transferring of functions to and from other departments. Until 1995, specific assistance for Aboriginal health was provided through the Aboriginal and Torres Strait Islander Commission, but with the change of government in March 1996, health issues for these people have come under the jurisdiction of the Department of Health and Family Services (DHFS).

There has been a trend to centralize services that coordinate aspects of health care delivery, but also some delegation of responsibility to regional and area authorities (AIHW 1998). At the local level, corporatized hospital boards administer most of the public acute hospitals. In New South Wales, executives responsible to area or district health boards manage health services, including hospitals. The regulation of private hospitals is at the state level, and 60 per cent of these are run by religious or charitable organizations as not-for-profit enterprises. While, historically, regulation of private hospitals was concerned with accommodation and safety issues, the focus is now on the quality of care, surgical overservicing and health planning (Palmer and Short 1994).

Professional and other pressure groups have an important influence on health policy developments. The Australian Medical Association (AMA) represents over half of all doctors, and maintains affiliations with many societies and colleges representing specialists. In comparison to doctors, nurses are less influential in the health policy-making process (Wall 1996).

Australia provides universal access to ambulatory and hospital care through a system of public insurance called Medicare. Medicare was established in 1984 and covers all people normally resident in Australia, with the exception of foreign diplomats and their dependants. Visitors from countries with which Australia has reciprocal health care agreements are covered in certain circumstances. The scheme is financed through general taxation and also by a 1.4 per cent levy on taxable income. The levy was initially set at 1 per cent, and though policy debate surrounds the Medicare levy, it finances less than 20 per cent of Medicare expenditure (Industry Commission 1997). Medicare was, in fact, a return to a national health insurance approach, which had been dismantled.

For over four decades, health policy in Australia has debated the respective merits of demerits of public versus private systems for finance and delivery. Medicare requires that individuals be given the choice of receiving public hospital services free of charge as public patients. The Health Insurance Act 1973 states that access to public hospitals is to be based on clinical need, and provision of services is to be geographically equitable. Since the introduction of Medicare, health care expenditures have increased as a proportion of GDP, from 7.6 per cent in 1996 to 8.4 per cent in 1997. Total public and private spending, estimated at A$43,204 million in 1996/97, representing A$2345 per person (AIHW 1998). Under a system known as bulk-billing, providers bill Medicare directly for 85 per cent of the scheduled fees, and forgo further payments. In 1997, more than 70 per cent of services were bulk-billed. There is an upper limit on patient co-payments per service and levels are reviewed annually. While providers are permitted to charge higher than the Medicare scheduled rate, with patients meeting the difference, in practice this occurs less than 20 per cent of the time.

Persons with public insurance receive care in public hospitals, while those with private insurance can access either private or public facilities. Private patients in both public and private hospitals are covered for 75 per cent of the scheduled fee, and the balance of costs can be met with private insurance or paid out-of-pocket. Because public hospitals receive payments from health insurance funds for private patient accommodation costs, they have incentives to accommodate private patients. The 1993, Medicare agreement aimed to address equity concerns about the crowding out of public patients by private patients by allowing some bonus funding for public admissions (De Abreu Lourenco *et al.* 1999).

Accident and emergency services and more specialized and technologically complex services are concentrated in the public system. Private insurance does not cover ambulatory medical services or fund any gaps between the Medicare rebate and fees which are charged, therefore individuals have incentives to use public facilities in order to avoid co-payments. Most private insurance is purchased by individuals rather than by employers, and the expenditure is not tax deductible (Peabody *et al.* 1996).

Hospital care is funded indirectly by payments to the state, under a per capita formula administered by the Commonwealth Grants Commission (Wheelwright 1995). The relationship between the Commonwealth and state governments promotes horizontal fiscal equalization and recognizes the differing revenue bases and expenditure demands of each state. State governments provide finance for capital spending and the recurrent funding of public hospitals. This includes per diem payments for each patient insured through Medicare but treated in a private hospital, maternity care centre, or receiving mental health services, as well as paying two-thirds of nursing home recurrent costs and geriatric care.

Commonwealth and state governments in 1995/96 financed 68.5 per cent of total health care expenditure, the balance coming from private insurance (10.5 per cent) and out-of-pocket payments (21 per cent). Since the introduction of Medicare in 1984 the private contribution to the total health budget has almost halved and individual payments have increased from 14.7 per cent to the current level of 20.9 per cent (De Abreu Lourenco *et al.* 1999).

Acute hospital care is responsible for 70 per cent of all admissions and 87.5 per cent of patient-days. Most other care is delivered by private providers and institutions. The expenditures of acute hospitals account for the largest percentage of health costs at 37.1 per cent of the national health budget, followed by medical services at 20.2 per cent and pharmaceuticals at 12.0 per cent (AIHW 1998: 167). In real terms the cost of health care more than doubled between 1975/76 and 1996/97, representing a real average annual increase of 3.5 per cent. If annual population growth is taken into account, real per-person health expenditure increased at an average rate of 2.2 per cent per year (AIWH 1998: 169). This increase in health service delivery costs is explained partly by an ageing population and increases in service utilization.

Doctors in the public system are usually salaried employees of hospitals or paid on a fee-per-session basis. In contrast, private doctors are usually reimbursed on a fee-for-service agreement in which the government sets a doctor's fee for Medicare (Peabody *et al.* 1996). Arrangements allow some specialists to work in both the public and private systems and to serve both public and private patients in public hospitals. Large hospitals may employ their own full-time medical staff with limited rights of practice. Teaching hospitals that contract their own staff and state funders are in a good position to exert some control over the private providers (Wall 1996). Diverse ownership arrangements for private hospitals include religious and philanthropic bodies, individual investors, business partnerships, registered companies and cooperative ownership structures.

The average length of stay in private hospitals is substantially lower than that in the public hospitals. This can be explained by the fact that the private hospitals largely complement the public system and provide immediate treatment for routine, non-complicated surgery. Most health care provision in Australia is private, the key exception being hospital infrastructure. A constitutional amendment in 1946 prohibited civil conscription, and this has prevented the development of a national health service such as occurred in the UK.

There is little integration of the public and private hospital sectors, although over the 1990s chains of public hospitals have become more common and ownership has become more concentrated. States are also experimenting with contracting-out public hospital care to private hospitals and privatizing public hospitals. Nursing homes are mainly privately owned, but are the subject of substantial government regulations which fix charges and regulate the number of beds. State governments are also responsible for licensing and there is substantial interstate variation in the quality of the accommodation provided.

Direct contracts between private health insurance funds and hospitals are not common, though the government is trying to encourage insurers to negotiate volume contracts directly with hospitals, and also moves towards preferred provider and managed care-type contracts. The medical professions, through the Australian Medical Association, have opposed such policies.

Pharmaceuticals are subsidized under the Pharmaceutical Benefits Scheme, which has existed since 1948. Co-payments were introduced in the 1980s; however, they are not covered by private health insurance. Various levels of co-payments exist, depending on age, income and health condition, and there is also a calendar year stop-loss.

In an effort to control rising pharmaceutical expenditures the government introduced a minimum pricing policy. It will not subsidize brand premiums, and allows generic substitution by pharmacists and indexing of the required co-payments. While Medicare funds some expenditure on dental and optometrical services, much of this is met through private funding.

General practitioners operate privately in sole practice or in partnerships. They are active in preventative medicine and act as gatekeepers to specialists and hospitals (Commonwealth Department of Health and Aged Care 1999). Access to GPs is good and this is reflected in high utilization rates (Abraham *et al.* 1995). An implementation programme is in force, called the Better Practice Programme, which rewards high quality general practices.

Proposals for reform

Since the introduction of Medicare in 1984, the government's share of health finance has grown to encompass two-thirds of all expenditure in health care: 68.5 per cent of state money comes from the Commonwealth, often in the form of tagged grants. The Commonwealth's ability to influence health policy through its disbursement of funds to states has been a controversial issue (Wheelwright 1995). A major reason for the growth of public expenditure is the fact that the Commonwealth has carried responsibility for open-ended areas of expenditure, such as medical services and pharmaceuticals.

The proportion of the population covered through private insurance fell from 68 per cent in 1982, to 50 per cent in 1984 and to 34.3 per cent in 1995. The rapid increase in the price of private insurance, and the advent of large co-payments and community rating systems are important factors contributing to this decline. Community rating means that private health insurance funds are vulnerable to adverse selection, and therefore the sick have strong incentives to take out cover. The effects have been greatest among the young and least among people aged over 50. Research has shown that the major beneficiaries of community rating are people with a high risk of hospitalization, the elderly (over 80 years), single people, and those in lower socio-economic groups (Schofield 1997). There is also some evidence that the incentives may not be delivering the desired results; for example, some families were being encouraged to purchase a low premium, high deductible insurance package, just to avoid paying the levy.

Since community rating promotes cross-subsidization by groups who use health services infrequently, its introduction had a major impact on the market for private health insurance and has particularly affected family membership units. Between 1984 and 1996, premium levels rose across the states in real terms by between 58 per cent and 173 per cent (AIHW 1998: 178). The sharpest decline in private insurance cover came from the top and middle income groups, while coverage among the lowest income group remained relatively constant between 1986 and 1995 (AIHW 1998: 180).

Despite this, spending in private hospitals increased to 8.2 per cent of non-capital health expenditure in 1995/96, a rise from 5.6 per cent in 1984/85. Private hospital admissions also increased 81 per cent, in contrast to a 46 per cent increase in hospital admissions in the public sector over that same ten-year period. This can be partially explained by the shift towards use of private facilities and changes to the case-mix being treated in private hospitals (Hall 1999: 98). For some procedures, such as eye or ear, nose and throat surgery, the proportion of patients receiving the service in private hospitals outstrips that in public hospitals.

In July 1997, the federal government introduced a tax rebate scheme worth A$1.5 billion aimed at stemming the movement away from private health insurance. This was designed to spread the high demand for hospital services that was putting pressure on some of the larger urban hospitals (Dow 1997). The incentives were focused on both low- and high-income groups. The scheme gave a tax rebate to low-income families who took out private health insurance, and also imposed a surcharge which penalized higher-income families not covered by private health insurance. The revenue from the surcharge was not put into the general revenue fund.

The incentives surrounding these policies were limited and did not succeed in reversing the decline in the take-up of private insurance. Most high-income earners already held private insurance policies, and the incentives for low-income earners were weak. Data collected by the Health Insurance Commission (HIC) in late 1997 showed that the downward trend in private health insurance coverage had stabilized and, indeed, was beginning to turn (Health Insurance Commission 1998).

The place of private insurance in the Australian health care system has been a contentious policy issue, and views differ as to whether private insurance should complement or compete with public finance through Medicare (Industry Commission 1997). The Commonwealth State Health Care Agreements recognize and support the significant role for the private sector in health care and the right of Australians to choose private care. The agreement also removed earlier provisions which entitled private and public patients to the same guaranteed access to public hospitals (Hall 1999).

In the May 1999 budget, the government announced that every Australian taking out private insurance will have 30 per cent of the premium paid by the Commonwealth, with no means test. The modifications will allow individuals to 'buy out' their Medicare cover and transfer it to private insurance, further supporting private insurance and lessening the fiscal pressures on the health vote (Hall 1999: 103). The government is proposing to develop lifetime community rating of insurance premiums, with a view to encouraging a long-term commitment to private insurance irrespective of periods of high need. Lifetime health cover will allow health funds to charge different premiums, depending on the age at which a person joins a health fund. Special provisions will be introduced to protect people over 65 and ensure that they can take out hospital cover at any time. The government is aiming to encourage greater participation in private insurance and is hoping to stabilize the system at roughly one-third of the population (Podger 1999: 112).

System impacts

There is a move to shift the focus from the funding of providers and health care inputs towards health outcomes. Lessons learned from coordinated care trials have shown considerable benefits from pooling all public health funds for identified specific population groups. Health Care Agreements now include conditions which facilitate the substitution of state hospital funds and Commonwealth medical and pharmaceutical funds where better health outcomes or efficiency gains can be demonstrated. This has fostered coordinated care arrangements, especially for those with chronic health problems (Podger 1999: 112).

Efficiency

Since the introduction of Medicare in 1984, Australia has utilized competition as a mechanism for promoting efficiency in the health sector. The success of this strategy has varied among states and territories. The measures can bring about only limited cost reductions and efficiency gains in isolation from other strategies. A desire for improved health and financial outcomes has promoted strategies for early disease intervention and greater emphasis on health promotion. The development of **case-mix funding** for hospitals has shifted the focus towards outcomes and consumers, has led to clearer accountability lines and more explicit internal costings, and has promoted efficiencies by reducing cost-shifting within hospitals (Podger 1999: 112). In spite of this, concerns have been raised about the possible consequences of case-mix funding on the quality of hospital care.

Open-ended funding arrangements for primary care mean that the government has limited capacity to keep expenditure on ambulatory care and pharmaceuticals under control. The Pharmaceutical

Benefits Scheme (PBS) has no capitation structures in relation to distribution volumes. Co-payments for prescriptions were introduced to try to control volumes. Commonwealth-sponsored trials are also being introduced to use GPs as notional fundholders, in the hope of overcoming some of the overservicing and poor coordination of health care services (Leeder 1998).

While public hospitals can exert pressure on the total costs of services delivered, without managed care arrangements and block contracts there are poor incentives for cost containment. Private insurance provides opportunities for the states to shift costs and compromise patient care by focusing on cost reductions rather than on quality or the most appropriate medical care (Wheelwright 1995). Subsidies on the costs of consultation and other inputs to primary care encourage providers to undervalue the resource, since they are remunerated by fee-for-service. The direct funding of public hospitals provides incentives for individuals to seek care directly from hospitals, though this is discouraged by using GPs as gatekeepers.

The present health care system leads to the overuse of certain services. Many hospital budgets are capped. However, despite active control of prices for general and specialist services, there is little constraint on the volume of treatments. A lack of coordination has led to oversupply of particular services and creates inefficiencies when patients move from one professional to another (Leeder 1998). The adoption of 'assignment' or bulk-billing agreements (when Medicare payment is accepted as payment in full) reduces administrative costs. The administration of health care in Australia represents over 3 per cent of total health expenditure and 12 per cent of the annual income contributions received by the funds (AIHW 1998: 175).

Figure 4.1 compares administrative costs in Australia with that in four other OECD countries. While the government has adopted strategies to subsidize private insurance and enhance competition, many of these policies have not achieved their objectives. For example, the government tried to foster competition by having the Health Insurance Commission operate a private insurance fund, Medicare Private; the effects have proved minimal. The use of community-rated premiums in the private insurance market has encouraged adverse selection and there have been associated efficiency losses for both private insurance and Medicare budgets. Medicare has provided not a safety net but a cheap alternative to private insurance (Sloan 1997).

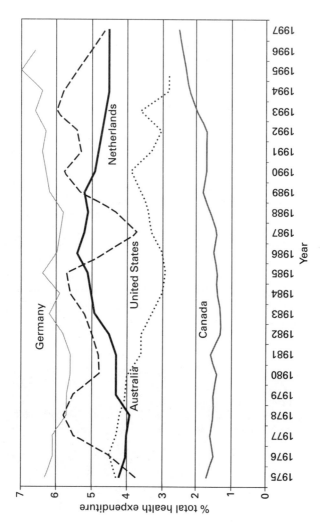

Figure 4.1 Expenditure on administration as a percentage of total health expenditure in five countries, 1975–97
Source: OECD (1999)

Cost containment

The main causes of rising health care expenditure in Australia are the Medical Benefits Scheme and the Pharmaceutical Benefits Scheme. Supply-side initiatives have dominated strategies used by both state and Commonwealth governments to minimize expenditure increases. Bulk-billing contracts are designed to attack the expenditure effects of both schemes. Other strategies have included restrictions on the number of new doctors who can claim Medicare reimbursements, and alternatives to fee-for-service payments (De Abreu Lourenco *et al.* 1999).

The increase in technological demands has brought increases to costs of health care delivery. However, little information at the Commonwealth level reveals the actual cost performance of the sector, particularly at the hospital level. Figures are available to calculate the cost per case-mix, related to the Australian national diagnosis related groups (AN-DRG), and has been used, especially in Victoria, to contain costs. New South Wales has adopted an alternative approach, of geographically-based administration which matches services to need. The average case-mix separation for acute hospital care for states and territories ranged from A$2261 in Victoria to A$3466 in the Australian Capital Territory. Nursing and medical staff costs fill a major component of these costs, equating to 46 per cent of the cost per case-mix adjusted separation (AIHW 1998: 191).

While global budgets promote cost containment, they have not succeeded in promoting productivity. To increase efficiency and productivity, some states have introduced output-related reimbursement programmes that link funding levels to case-mix adjustment discharges and reductions in elective surgery waiting times (Peabody *et al.* 1996).

Attempts at cutting the costs of Medicare have met resistance from the general public; for example, in 1991, when the then Labour government introduced user charges for GP services, a move opposed by welfare and women's groups and by backbenchers. The policy was soon reversed. The same fate met the proposal to introduce gap insurance to cover the difference between actual costs and the Medicare subsidy (Gray 1996).

Equity

The introduction of Medicare was motivated by the goal of purchasing equitable access to government-funded health care. Medicare provides a safety net for people who cannot afford the out-of-pocket costs of private insurance. At the same time, Medicare's universality does not ensure the same ease of access and cost of use for everyone for all services (Hall 1999: 107).

Diverse arrangements across the states mean that a degree of geographical inequity is inherent in the system. Each state has a specific agreement with the Commonwealth government for the provision of health services. These agreements specify rural and remote areas to ensure provision of reasonable public access to a basic range of hospital services. Ongoing policy challenges surround equity and access issues for lower-income groups, rural and remote populations and indigenous people.

Within Medicare there are some differentials which act to channel assistance to particular groups. For example, the purchasing of approved PBS-listed pharmaceutical items is set to A$20, but individuals holding concession cards issued by the Department of Social Security pay only A$3.20. In 1996/97, A$2333 million was spent on PBS prescription items, of which A$1867 million was spent in subisidizing cardholders (De Abreu Lourenco *et al.* 1999).

Financing arrangements for Medicare result in considerable redistribution towards those with higher servicing requirements, and figures show that the average number of visits to general practitioners and specialists has increased. While partly explained by the ageing population, the trends also reflect growth in the number of practising primary care staff, and greater emphasis on health care in areas such as immunization, pap smears and general health check-ups (AIHW 1998).

Australia's fragmented health care system has failed to provide adequate care for the Aboriginal people. Health surveys reveal that Aboriginal people suffer significantly more health problems than non-indigenous adults, including high rates of heart-related conditions, high blood pressure and diabetes. Aboriginal people are classified as high-risk because of drinking, heavy smoking and obesity. Reflecting their low socio-economic position in Australian society, only 11 per cent of Aboriginal people hold any private insurance (Loff and Cordner 1999). Proposals to target indigenous health care include the recruitment and training of people to work especially in indigenous health (Commonwealth Department of Health and Aged Care 1999). Recent Aboriginal health care strategies have focused on self-determination and management, and on dealing with the wider environmental issues of the Aboriginal community.

Choice

Health care support is focused primarily on the services of general practitioners and specialists, and choice of other providers is limited. General practitioners act as gatekeepers for specialists who, in turn, provide referrals for hospital care, since few GPs have admitting privileges (Peabody *et al.* 1996). Private patients who receive service in public hospitals have choice of provider, while public patients do not. Medicare was designed to ensure access to public hospitals, as well as general and specialist care; however, growing waiting lists that block immediate access to health care treatments are common under the current system (AIHW 1998). Access to emergency care is still excellent (Leeder 1998).

The Australian government has seen competition as a key means of enhancing efficiency. It also recognizes that some controls on competition are required to protect minimum levels of quality and standards of service. However, the accuracy of information relating to levels of hospital quality is hard to analyse as each state manages data independently, making it difficult to impose a national set of standards.

Conclusion

Many of the difficulties facing the Australian health care system arise from the complex and sometimes fragmented relationships between Commonwealth, state, local government and private sectors groups. System performance would benefit from the removal of some of the barriers between the public and private sectors, and strategies are needed to encourage better management and use of resources. More professional involvement and engagement in the policy process is needed, which brings together users, providers, purchasers and funders of health care to develop reform strategies which improve health outcomes.

Australia's efforts at limiting technology expansion, hospital budgets and doctor charges are important examples for other countries wishing to stabilize health care costs. So too are its experiences with the growth in primary care visits, high rates of hospitalization and lengthening waiting lists for non-emergency care.

Australia's strategies are directed towards reducing costs and improving coordination and management, with a view to improved health outcomes. Problems persist for specific population groups, such as the Aboriginal and lower socio-economic groups. Better strategic management of information and resources is needed, and policy debate that views the system more holistically at local, state and Commonwealth levels of governance.

Current government policy intentions which involve shifting the burden of health care expenditure from the public to the private system are strategies which warrant greater international attention. So far, efforts to increase private health insurance have not been effective, and it is not clear whether policies will have their intended effect of reducing resource pressures on the public system. The Australian reform experiences highlight the growing importance of private sector business interests and the not-for-profit sector in the finance and delivery of services. The involvement of private sector groups in medical services and particularly diagnostic services means that the private sector is a critical element of the national health system. The growth of large corporates as service providers receiving state funding is changing the complexion of the system from former times when services were largely the domain of individual practitioners operating in private practice. Future directions for the system are hard to predict and a key issue will be the degree to which there is a significant shift of funding towards private insurance. In the area of provision, various alternatives exist, including that the private sector will increase its role in delivering public hospital services under contract to state governments. Most important, however, the Australian experience demonstrates that policy-makers and the public will need to think more broadly in terms of the options and opportunities for public and private involvement:

> In considering reform options, governments will find that the traditional and usually ideological dichotomies of public versus private or insurance versus Medicare are unhelpful in finding solutions. The shifting balance of public and private sector roles, together with changing patterns of health care delivery, rising community expectations and intergenerational issues of financing health care for an ageing population will require new paradigms. (Foley, in Bloom 2000: 114)

5

ROLES AND INTERFACES: UNITED KINGDOM AND NEW ZEALAND

In many respects, the health care systems of the United Kingdom (UK) and New Zealand have much in common, both historically and in terms of recent approaches to reform. The New Zealand system evolved along British lines, including a reliance on tax funding, the public ownership of hospitals, and the use of self-employed GPs as gatekeepers to specialist and other services. Private insurance exists in both countries, largely as a supplement to the public insurance system, and covers the cost of treatment in private hospitals and, in the UK only, dedicated private 'pay-beds' in public hospitals. Relative to the UK, patient co-payments in New Zealand for primary medical care are substantial, and some subsidies for GP services are aimed at specific groups.

Traditionally, both the UK and New Zealand operated an integrated model of purchasing and provision at the hospital level. In the 1990s, both countries introduced a purchaser–provider split, involving competition among public and private providers, an opportunity which was taken up to a greater degree in New Zealand than in the UK. The UK purchaser–provider split largely involved internal markets, which operated mostly in a public sector setting. The 1993 New Zealand reforms introduced a purchaser–provider split shaped by proposals for managed competition in the Netherlands.

Both countries explored and experimented with the purchase of managed (integrated) care packages. The UK initiatives were firmly based around general practitioners, while the New Zealand integrated care pilots related to specific services or parts of services.

The election of the Labour government in the UK in 1997 and a coalition Labour–Alliance government in New Zealand in 1999 has led to further restructuring and changes to the roles and interfaces of public and private organizations.

UNITED KINGDOM

The UK health care system has a reputation for giving value for money, enjoying health status indicators similar to those in many other industrialized countries but lower expenditure levels (OECD 1992: 119) than in other countries. Expenditure has grown as a percentage of GDP from 5.9 per cent in 1986 to 6.9 per cent in 1998.

The health system has been shaped by the National Health Service (NHS), a public institution established to ensure universal access to comprehensive health services. The four principles guiding the NHS are that access to health services should be universal, comprehensive, 'free at the point of delivery' to the patient, and financed primarily through general tax revenues. The NHS has maintained its pre-eminent position over the total system, despite many substantial changes since 1948 to the structure and roles of public and private organizations engaged in the funding, purchasing and provision of health care.

Public and private roles

Funding of health care in the UK derives from six main sources: general taxation, National Insurance contributions, patient charges, income generation, private medical insurance and direct payments. Public funding relies primarily on general taxation (84 per cent), payroll taxes (13 per cent) and direct payments (3 per cent). Private insurance and private health care have played a small but important role in the health care system. Private care delivers greater convenience for the patient, choice of doctor, and standards of comfort and privacy. As in New Zealand, private insurance allows individuals with the ability to obtain quicker access to specialist care and to non-acute surgery. Private insurance is supplied by competing non-profit insurers and covers about 11 per cent of the population. Premiums for individuals are related to age, rising steeply for elderly people (OECD 1992: 116). The bulk of subscribers are higher-paid employees and the self-employed, with around half of subscribers in group schemes (where employers pay premiums) which are experience-rated. As of 1996, there were 25 private health insurers, of which 7 were non-profit provident associations.

Although private insurance coverage may be held on top of NHS coverage, individuals must still make tax contributions to the NHS, even if they go private. The public funding arrangements ensure that potential users pool their risks across the whole population, and the system redistributes from low risk to high risk. The government sets the amount of funding for the NHS. Finance is allocated prospectively, with only limited adjustment made for the actual level of activity undertaken. Separate funding allocations are made for England, Scotland, Wales and Northern Ireland. There have always been differences in services; however, from 1999, political and legislative powers have been devolved to the Scottish Parliament and the Welsh Assembly with implications for the provision of health services across the UK. The discussions below focus on arrangements in England.

Traditionally, funding arrangements in England have centred around two major budgets: one for family health services and one for hospital and community health services, the latter comprising about two-thirds of total expenditure (OECD 1992). The family health services budgets were demand-driven, and levels were based on forecasts of spending needs. Family practitioners work in the NHS as independent contractors, and primary care budgets include expenditures on drugs. Sometimes supplementary allocations were required during a year to meet unexpected changes in volume or prices, though various controls were applied to the price and volume of services (OECD 1992: 116). Speciality and hospital care, and part of the community, home and mental health services budget were fixed, and based on the previous year's budget with allowances for the size, age and health of the resident population. The remainder of community services came under the authority of local town budgets, which were not part of the NHS.

Primary care in the UK has always been based on enrolment with a private, self-employed GP, over whom individuals have free choice. The GP is the patient's initial point of contact with the health system, and governs referrals to specialists. Prior to reform in the 1990s, the primary care sector was administered by Family Practitioner Committees (FPCs), which were directly funded by the Department of Health and included GPs, dentists and pharmacists. Local government provided community services, such as nursing homes, home care for elderly people, and other support services.

Government subsidy for GP services comprised a base salary to cover the fixed costs of operating a practice, capitation payments (equivalent to about half of a GP's income) reflecting the number of patients in the practice, and fees for certain procedures like vaccinations and tests (Graig 1991: 223). GPs could earn more than the average by providing additional fee-paid services or by attracting above-average numbers of patients. If above-average expenses were incurred, GPs met the costs themselves. Conversely, if below-average expenses were incurred, the savings could be kept (OECD 1992: 117). This arrangement provided some incentives for GPs to underservice patients and to provide fee-based services, though neither underservicing nor overservicing of patients have been considered to be prevalent (Barr 1990: 76).

Pharmacists were paid dispensing fees for prescriptions, on a sliding scale that tapered according to the volume of prescriptions. These fees were paid out of a global sum negotiated with the Department of Health by the pharmacists' representative body. Pharmacists received 5 per cent of the net ingredient cost of medicines. Drug prices themselves were regulated by a pharmaceutical price regulation scheme.

The 1980s and early 1990s saw the development of more formal approaches to contracting and greater emphasis on good management practice, including the introduction of general management throughout the NHS as recommended in the Griffiths Report (Griffiths 1983). In the late 1980s, resources became constrained on the supply side, leading to concerns about underfunding. New initiatives were introduced including increasing the number of NHS pay-beds in public hospitals, charging for car parking, and the renting of space within hospitals to shops and businesses. Yet little altered in a fundamental way the power and influence of hospitals and their clinicians over patients and their GPs.

The NHS hospital system comprises three tiers: community hospitals, district general hospitals, and tertiary hospitals offering secondary care and highly specialized services. There are approximately 230 independent medical/surgical hospitals in the UK, with five main groups accounting for just over 60 per cent of hospitals and a combined share of approximately 65 per cent of total private beds. Successive governments in the 1990s were concerned to improve the quality of NHS services and fostered the Private Finance Initiative, a partnership programme designed to encourage private investment in the public sector. Private long-term care was also encouraged.

In 1990, the Audit Commission extended its brief from local government to the NHS, leading to value-for-money studies and other recommendations and strategies for greater efficiency. In the same year, a national GP contract was introduced setting out in terms the expectations regarding services to be delivered. As part of a much broader agenda of public sector reform, the Conservative government conducted a review of the NHS in 1988/89. The review was motivated by public concern about the funding and performance of the health service, including the closing of hospital wards and the cancellation of operations. While the NHS maintained considerable public support, there was a widely-held view within the government that public services were inefficient, lacked responsiveness to users and were subject to 'provider capture' by the professional groups.

In 1989, the government released reform proposals in the White Paper *Working for Patients*, and in 1990 enacted the NHS and Community Care Act. The changes brought modifications to the health care system in the areas of funding, purchasing and provision of care. There is evidence that the possibility of shifting the funding of the NHS from general taxation to private insurance was considered; however, support for the NHS has always been extremely high among the general public. Following a leaked Cabinet paper which considered the likely political consequences of a shift to private insurance, the prime minister, Mrs Thatcher, found herself under pressure to reassure the public that: 'The NHS is safe with us' (Ranade 1998: 103). Thereafter, the reforms were largely confined to issues surrounding the purchasing and provision of care.

Proposals for reform

The health reforms were part of a larger comprehensive economic and social policy agenda which promoted a more competitive economy, lower public expenditures and taxes, a reduction in welfare dependency and opportunities for greater individual choice regarding social services. The reforms introduced modifications to both the function and structure of organizations. These measures served to challenge the very essence and ethos of the NHS as a public institution.

At the time of the reforms, the purchasing and delivery of care fell into three broad categories: hospital care, primary care, and community/social services and long-term care. Within the hospital sector, there were 14 regional health authorities (RHAs), each of which had responsibility for 4–5 million people. Each RHA was divided into approximately 15 district health authorities (DHAs), making a total of nearly 200 DHAs, with four or five hospitals reporting to each DHA. The hospital sector had a cash-limited budget, and resources were designed making use of a formula which took into account the age and mortality rates of the population served.

A key design feature was the establishment of a purchaser–provider split. Pre-reform, the DHAs had responsibility for both planning and operating health services, apart from general practice. Post-reform, hospitals and community services became self-governing NHS trusts. DHAs were given budgets on the basis of a weighted capitation formula, instructed to assess the needs of their resident populations and asked to purchase appropriate levels of acute and community health care from public and private institutions. GPs were given the option of becoming fundholders and assigned budgets to purchase selected services on behalf of their patients, including diagnostic services, elective surgery and outpatient care. The scheme grew rapidly and by 1998 there were 3500 GP fundholders.

The reforms allowed private hospitals and facilities to compete with public institutions for services and expanded opportunities and incentives for private finance to flow into private health insurance and capital expenditure. Tax deductibility for private insurance purchased by the elderly was also introduced. Key goals of the reforms were efficiency and greater patient choice, although providers still held the key to determining the nature and locus of care. The phrase 'dictated competition' was used to describe the competitive forces which were unleashed by the reforms. The changes were described as establishing an 'internal' or quasi-market arising from the assumption that much of the purchasing and providing remained within the NHS, although this was no longer accurate as purchasers could obtain services from both private and public providers. The principal NHS purchaser remained the DHAs, along with a new type of purchaser, the GP fundholder. These GP purchasers established contracts for the delivery of care with any provider or institution, whether public or private.

Figure 5.1 portrays the changes which resulted in purchasing being done by two groups: DHAs and GP service providers. The development of GP fundholding provisions was a late addition to

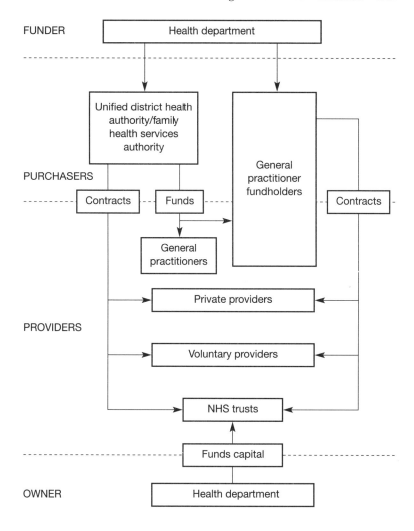

Figure 5.1   Health reforms in the United Kingdom
Source: Mason and Morgan (1995)

the reforms, resulting in both DHAs and GPs taking on a purchasing role. In order to qualify, GPs had to have a practice population of at least 11,000 patients, and schemes contained a provision that limited the financial risk on the GP fundholder. If a patient was found to be costing more than £5000 in hospital treatment in any one year, the extra costs were to be met by a contingency fund held by the DHA (Glennerster and Matsaganis 1994: 237). Such a policy was essential to reduce the incentives for providers to cream-skim. The first Patient's Charter was published in January 1992 and a revised version in 1995. Although the second charter extended the standards to include things such as food and children's needs, the focus was still on waiting times. Concerns were expressed that: 'the pressure to achieve targets linked to a relatively narrow set of indicators would distract staff's attention from other issues, notably the quality, effectiveness and appropriateness of the care given' (Radical Statistics Health Group 1995: 1048).

In April 1993, opportunities for local purchasing were expanded to include community services such as district nursing, health visiting, mental health care, services for people with learning disabilities, chiropody and dietetics. At the same time, the Department of Health made a decision that GP fundholder allocations should be 'partly linked to a weighted capitation formula'. Concerns were expressed that this would encourage cream-skimming (Matsaganis and Glennerster 1994: 33).

In October 1994, further measures were taken which aimed to increase the number of GP fundholders and to increase the range of services that fundholders could buy (Propper 1995: 78). Fundholding was extended to three categories (Drummond 1995: 38):

- Community fundholding, an option for smaller practices with more than 300 patients, which excludes all acute hospital treatments but includes practice expenses and drugs.
- Standard fundholding, the initial option, but the list size reduced to 5000.
- Total purchasing, an option whereby GPs in a locality would purchase all hospital and community care for their patients.

The reforms were also directed at the accountability of the health care systems. Critics commented on the limited accountability by consultants for the quality of care delivered; poor information about the activities of GPs and on the cost-effectiveness of various treatments; and the incidence of large, unexplained variations in clinical practice (Light 1992: 150). Emphasis was given to the need for better data and systems to inform market choices and to monitor contract performance. The reforms costed capital for the first time, and every NHS facility received an appraised value and was then charged an annual proportionate amount per square yard

(Light 1992: 149, 152). Changes to service delivery, medical audit and management processes were introduced as strategies for improving both the quality and efficiency of service delivery.

The district health authorities and family health services authorities were merged into single health authorities in 1996, as part of measures to coordinate primary and secondary care. A large number of innovative arrangements evolved to cover purchasing arrangements. Consortia developed and fundholding practices worked together and in various arrangements with health authorities. Total purchasing pilots allowed groups of fundholders to come together to purchase a substantial range of hospital and community services. New variants of purchasing evolved and, by 1997, over half the population was covered by fundholding practices, which controlled over 10 per cent of hospital and community services (LeGrand *et al.* 1998: 11).

Following the election of the Labour government in 1997, further modifications to the organization of the health system were made, as outlined in *The New NHS* (Secretary of State for Health 1997). An implementation timeframe of ten years was announced and there is an expectation of significant management savings. Happening in the year which marked the fiftieth anniversary of the NHS, these changes were no less than the fifth major reorganization in the NHS since 1975 (Klein 1998). The reforms replace GP fundholding, competition and the internal market by 481 primary care groups (PCGs) which will undertake total purchasing for individuals, thus eliminating the role of health authorities in commissioning services. PCGs will be much larger than previous primary care-based approaches, with populations ranging from 46,000 to 257,000, and it is expected that they will progress through four developmental stages, culminating in the formation of primary care trusts. Level 1 is where the PCG acts as an advisory committee to the health authority; level 2 where it takes devolved responsibility for managing the budget and is formally part of the health authority; level 3 involves the PCG becoming a free-standing body accountable to the health authority for commissioning care; and level 4 extends its responsibilities to the provision of community health services. It is envisaged that most PCGs will begin at level 2 and that all will work closely with local government social services departments, health authorities and with NHS trusts. As PCGs take on responsibility for commissioning services, the health authorities will shift their role towards strategic planning.

One important feature of this latest round of reforms is the development of new approaches to public health. While a 1992 White Paper, *The Health of the Nation*, developed a national public health strategy for England for the first time, the approach was criticized for placing undue emphasis on individual behaviours to explain poor health and ignoring important social determinants, including inequality and poverty. A White Paper *Saving Lives: Our Healthier Nation*, was published in July 1999 to outline a public health strategy and 26 health action zones (HAZs), representing areas of particular social and economic deprivation, were targeted for attention. The span of policies which will be adopted by HAZs is wide and will include strategies surrounding housing, employment and other areas critical to improving health outcomes and will involve partnerships with the voluntary sector and with industry.

The Labour government's strategy for health reform has been described as a 'third way', representing a balance between the command and control strategies and more competitive internal market approaches to reform. The rhetoric is that the latest reforms have displaced the internal market and replaced competition by cooperation. Yet several elements of the earlier reforms remain, including the purchaser–provider split. Measures to foster greater cooperation, including the development of long-term contracts, will offer protection for both good and not-so-good provider organizations. The third way has been described as 'a cocktail of different approaches', aimed at synthesizing approaches often regarded as exclusive, such as centralization and local autonomy, the use of sanctions and incentives, reliance on planning and sanctions, and devolution, involving incentives and competition (Ham 1999).

Health authorities will continue to exist and be responsible for setting PCG budgets, assessing health needs, drawing up health improvement programmes developed in partnership with all of the local interests and deciding on the range and location of health care services for their residents. The latest proposals have shifted the rhetoric towards increasing consistency and equity of treatment across the service, and this is likely to increase standardization relative to the previous arrangements. There is debate about whether previous arrangements were, in fact, unfair, being merely the result of the different capacity and efficiency of GP fundholders.

The reforms have also focused on improving the quality of care and ensuring that there are relatively uniform service standards across the country. Confidence in the quality of NHS services was eroded by a number of high-profile events, including tragedies surrounding pediatric heart surgery at Bristol and cancer-screening failures at Kent hospitals. The latest changes include provision for evidence-based national service frameworks for major care areas and disease groups, a National Institute for Clinical Excellence to promote clinical guidelines and good practice, and a Commission for Health Improvement to monitor quality in the delivery of services. Clinical governance is being introduced to make hospital chief executives responsible for quality. Health authorities are being asked to improve health outcomes, as well as overseeing the delivery of health services, and to give greater attention to the social and economic determinants of health. Focus is to be placed on building relationships between PCGs and local authorities in recognition of the latter's potential to influence the socio-economic environment and their role in the delivery of community services.

System impacts

In reviewing the impact of the reforms on policy goals, emphasis is placed on the reforms introduced by the Conservative government under Mrs Thatcher. Several excellent reviews exist of the impact of the Thatcher reforms, including Robinson and Le Grand (1994), Klein *et al.* (1996) and Le Grand *et al.* (1998). Measuring impacts is problematic since no systematic evaluation was undertaken of the substantial institutional changes. The pace and scale of change and the absence of a baseline has made it difficult to separate out the impacts arising from system changes from other influences.

Efficiency

A chief criticism of the pre-1988 NHS was that it exhibited both allocative and technical inefficiency. The system experienced rising costs, increasing numbers of tasks, greater variability among parts of the service, notable deficiencies, overstaffing, and marked regional inequalities (Madden 1991). Donaldson and Mooney (1993) criticized the service for being unresponsive to particular groups, such as the mentally ill and the elderly, and for being unaware of the implications of policy choices on resources outside the NHS budget. Costs were shifted to patients and to local authority services, such as the home help services.

A contributing factor to the inefficiency was the absence of a single funding stream, which allowed resources to be shifted between primary and secondary care. The fragmentation created incentives for budget-constrained physicians to shift patients, and thereby costs, from their budgets onto other parts of the system. For example, NHS hospital decision-makers had incentives to shift drug costs onto the primary care system. Since hospitals used cheap generic drugs while GPs prescribed expensive branded drugs, this situation increased the NHS drugs bill with no significant benefits in patient welfare (Maynard 1991).

Hospitals received global budgets that were set historically, with additions for expected rises in pay and prices and planned improvements in services, and with deductions for planned efficiency improvements (OECD 1992). Hospitals that made cost-savings could not carry these savings over to the next year's budget. The use of block budgets and lack of price signals fostered the attitude among providers that resources, including capital assets, were free goods.

General practitioners were remunerated mainly on a capitation basis, thus reducing the incentives on providers to oversupply created by fee-for-service type reimbursement arrangements. While, in theory, capitation gives GPs an incentive to retain patients on their lists, there remains a clear preference for patients who are low risk and low cost. Capitation payments have the potential to encourage providers to lower their standard of care by reducing the length of consultations, prescribing more, or referring more patients to hospital. However, the capitation system does provide GPs with greater scope to shift their treatment from curative care to health promotion and prevention activities.

Pre-reform, GPs had few incentives to restrain referrals to outpatient departments or referrals for elective surgery, since they did not bear the costs of such activity. GPs also had an open-ended drugs budget, providing an incentive to prescribe freely to patients and to medicalize their conditions. Providers dominated the allocation of services in accordance with perceived clinical need rather than patient preferences (OECD 1994). The reforms aimed to improve incentives for efficiency and to impose measures to control the NHS drugs bill.

The first year under the new system produced a 5.6 per cent increase in the number of in-patients treated. It was suggested, however, that this had little to do with the reforms because they had not yet had time to take effect (Pallot 1992). A serious confounding factor was that system reforms were introduced at a time when the level of resources to the NHS was increased substantially. In the four years prior to the 1991 reforms, real NHS spending rose by 13 per cent, while in the four years after the reforms the planned real terms increase was 26 per cent (Glennerster and Matsaganis 1994: 241). Changes in the way that procedures were recorded were also made about this time, which led to difficulties in measuring impacts. Up until 1987/88, people were counted each time they were discharged; however, in 1988/89 inpatients were counted each time they changed consultant or specialist within a hospital, and figures were expressed in terms of finished consultant episodes. Since funding was based on finished consultant episodes, some suggested that all episodes, however short, were being recorded and that this led to the observed increase in throughput (Radical Statistics Health Group 1995: 1045). Another change was to classify healthy babies born in hospital as in-patients.

Many aspects of the reforms were adopted by self-selection; units approved as trusts were self-selected, then selected again by the secretary of state using various criteria such as managerial competence, the level of computerization and the credibility of their business plans. GP fundholders were also self-selecting: first they had to be interested and then they had to fulfil certain criteria set out by the Department of Health.

The quasi-market arrangements placed pressure on providers to become more efficient, for fear of losing customers, though the reforms still let medical providers determine the nature of services to be received. The empowerment of GPs was important and provided incentives for them to shift care from the hospital to primary care settings. Gains were achieved in the form of improved communication and coordination between hospitals and primary care providers.

Somewhat unexpectedly, the GP fundholders became a positive feature of the reforms and set the stage for the move to managed care and PCGs which were to follow under the Labour government. There are several factors that explain the success of GP fundholding. Being voluntary, the scheme could secure the support of GPs who were motivated to make the scheme work. GPs were able to purchase services on behalf of their patients, to be innovative in selecting services and service providers and to utilize savings to provide additional care. In contrast, health authorities were required to purchase the same services and could not keep surpluses.

The reforms encouraged more private sector health financing and provision, as well as the introduction of market and management principles into the NHS. Greater competition resulted from encouraging private providers and competition among NHS

GPs, hospitals and trusts. Separation of the purchaser and provider roles within the NHS made it easier to identify what services were being traded, by whom, at what price and quality. The information created by these trading processes promoted efficiency by identifying opportunities for gain and restructuring trading relationships (Maynard 1991: 1281).

An important reform element was the clarification of the purchaser role. The open needs-based purchasing made service deficiencies more transparent and there were early claims that improvements had been achieved in the allocation of resources (Light 1992: 154). Efficiency gains resulted from the closer integration of primary and hospital care. GPs were able to refer their patients to any hospital they chose, while local purchasers placed contracts with providers and ensured that GPs' patients used the services. If, however, patients were referred to providers not contracted to the local purchaser, NHS money followed the patients and the health authorities found themselves in financial difficulties. Hence, the reforms provided a strong incentive for purchasers to identify and meet GP preferences (Maynard 1991: 1281).

Allocative efficiency was reduced by political constraints designed to minimize the consequences of reform in marginal constituencies, and by a lack of data to inform market exchanges (Maynard 1991: 1285). Restrictions on competition served to undermine the potential for allocative efficiency. Allocative efficiency over geographical regions was difficult to achieve because of problems arising from working across district boundaries to match treatment cases with spare capacity (Redwood 1988: 17). There is disagreement regarding the degree to which access to private provision did assist allocative efficiency. While Higgins claimed, on one hand, that the private sector absorbed some of the excess demand for health services that the NHS could not fulfil, private sector activity did not reduce NHS waiting lists (Higgins 1988: 236).

It is likely that the structural reforms had mixed effects on allocative efficiency. GP fundholding forced doctors to consider the costs of their referral decisions, by giving them a budget with which to buy some services for their patients. It encouraged GPs to carry out minor surgery themselves and to purchase from hospitals offering lower-cost service, which would improve allocative efficiency. However, GPs also faced incentives to under-refer patients to hospitals, in order to stay within budget or to make savings.

Chadda (1995a: 5) reports an investigation that was ordered to explain a marked increase (14.4 per cent in one region) of emergency referrals. Initial findings revealed that GP fundholders had referral rates which were four times those of GPs. GP fundholders competed with health authorities as purchasers and this had the potential to reduce efficiency (Ham 1992). One of the concerns regarding the development of GP fundholding was that this development occurred at the expense of the health authority, and limited its ability to influence the balance between 'emergency versus elective care' (Ranade 1994: 160). GP fundholders were 'prepared to choose new suppliers and/or change the nature of the product they bought' (Propper 1995: 79). This change led to other providers also making changes. GP fundholders were very effective in most cases, proving able to control, and to contain to within 2–3 per cent of their budgets, the patient flows to hospital (Glennerster and Matsaganis 1994: 240).

In the three years to 1994, fundholders saved £117.7 million from their budgets (Chadda 1995b: 8). It is unclear what effect this has had, but one in four fundholders is known to have underspent by £100,000. 'In one fundholding practice, GPs had used part of the practice's £30,000 savings to set up a shop selling kitchen equipment' (Chadda 1995c: 3). Fundholder regulations were amended in April 1995 to make it a requirement that fundholders consider value for money in purchasing; however, they were not required to return any underspending, nor were they required to redirect this into patient services.

The reforms did add considerably to administration costs. GP fundholders were required individually to bill services to patients, and hospitals had to closely monitor their patients. If consultants had 'too many' patients from one DHA and not enough from another, they might not get paid. GP fundholding practices were thought to be spending an extra 2–3 per cent of their budget on administration (Glennerster and Matsaganis 1994: 243). It is likely that some of this administration resulted in improved monitoring of care and gains in efficiency.

Greater freedom was given to providers (notably NHS trusts) to manage. Trusts used their new power to improve efficiency, citing increases in activity and reductions in waiting times and lengths of stay (OECD 1992: 128). In the early stages, reforms provided little freedom for entrepreneurial development since trusts were constrained by the pricing rules. Three fundamental rules applied, namely that prices should be based on costs; costs should generally be arrived at on a full-cost basis; and there should be no planned cross-subsidization between contracts. Trusts were able to set a price equal to marginal cost only when they had unplanned excess capacity (Drummond 1995: 57). Over time, the trusts became more responsive to the new incentives provided by the reformed NHS environment. With their new managerial freedom, trusts coped with excess demand by adjusting prices and offering non-NHS purchasers the chance to buy surplus capacity. For instance, Manchester's Christie Hospital offered purchasers the option of shorter waiting times in return for higher treatment prices. However, whether this produced gains in allocative efficiency must be judged in terms of the opportunity cost of the higher prices, since purchasers now had less to spend on other services (Appleby 1992: 136–7).

In many regions the competitive provider model did not exist at the secondary level, because a monopoly provider delivered the range of services. In cases where a monopsony purchaser also existed, the bargaining outcome was uncertain and depended on the relative negotiating strengths of the two market players. Furthermore, in London, where the potential for competition was greatest, the government postponed the creation of hospital trusts prior to the 1992 general election (Shackley and Healey 1993: 160–1).

General practitioners who were part of fundholding arrangements had stronger incentives for allocative and technical efficiency than those who were not fundholders. Fundholding provided GPs with incentives to be innovative and to substitute more effective care for their patients. Some suggested that increasing the capitation component of doctors' pay may have had a negative impact on allocative efficiency by inducing them to add more patients to their lists and to carry out unvalidated screening procedures which diverted resources from more effective activities. The reforms had the potential to divert GPs from clinical activity by requiring them to negotiate contracts and undertake a managerial role (Light 1992: 162). Some denied the ability of the internal market to increase the power of consumers, and suggested that, at best, GPs aimed to address the needs of the collectivity of patients (Donaldson and Mooney 1993).

Technical efficiency is an area where the new style of NHS organization appears to have had some success. Before the reforms, there were numerous variations in cost and efficiency across districts in the service. Marked differences in productivity existed among providers at all levels, but there were few incentives to save, since funds not spent by due dates could not be carried over

(Madden 1991: 381). Some technical efficiency gains were attained in two ways.

First, there were mergers of DHAs, and second, providers such as GPs formed consortia to maximize their bargaining power with other providers and to reduce administrative costs (Ranade 1994: 155). Collaborative arrangements between health authorities and family health services authorities took place to achieve economies of scale, centralization of skills and greater financial leverage (Oakley and Greaves 1995: 31). Some gains were made with the waiting lists. While there was little overall reduction in the median value of waiting times between 1988 and 1993, there has been a dramatic reduction in numbers of people waiting over 18 months (Radical Statistics Health Group 1995: 1045).

In response to criticism that waiting time could easily be influenced by time waiting for a first outpatient appointment, new statistics were collected on the waiting time for the first appointment at outpatients. National standards were introduced stating that 90 per cent of people should have their first appointment within 13 weeks and all within 26 weeks. Initial data indicated that 83 per cent of patients waited 13 weeks and 96 per cent less than 26 weeks (Radical Statistics Health Group 1995: 1047).

Cost containment

The NHS has system design features that have made it successful relative to other systems in the area of cost containment. In particular, the high level of public funding and control over budgets has assisted efforts to contain total costs. Other factors include the limitations placed on the NHS's provision of high-technology medicine and elective surgery, and the fact that the NHS has considerable market power as an almost monopsonist buyer of medical supplies (Griffith *et al.* 1987: 234).

The Thatcher reforms allowed further constraints on health care budgets. The resource management initiative was designed to increase awareness of resource constraints in clinical decision-making. Cost-containment measures included indicative prescribing budgets for GPs, which were previously open-ended. The share of GP remuneration based on fee-for-service was reduced, with a view to reducing the tendency for services to be oversupplied. Global budgeting for hospitals was also retained.

The incentive given to private insurance coverage was related to the goal of public sector cost containment, as was the 1992 Private Finance Initiative (PFI) which provided incentives for private finance to fund schemes in health and other sectors. The PFI, established by the Treasury, required trusts to demonstrate that they had sought private finance before applying for funding through government sources, making private finance the preferred method of paying for capital projects (Ham 1995: 415). The emphasis was placed on using private finance not only for the cost of new building but also for the provision of associated services. The trusts took the lead role in these ventures and this served to 'alleviate concerns that the NHS is turning over its core business to private hands without public debate on the long-term implications' (Brown *et al.* 1995: 19). Treasury rules required that schemes funded under the PFI should involve a genuine transfer of risk to the private sector in order to justify the returns that might be generated (Ham 1995: 416). It was hard to imagine that the private sector would wish to assume this risk without also wanting significant influence over the management of the investment.

The White Paper reforms mandated increases in spending on management and administrative staff, premises improvement, and investment in information technology (Madden 1991: 391). From 1989 to 1993, 30,000 new staff were employed in the NHS in management, administrative and clerical roles. Whether these extra resources allocated to the NHS increased the administrative efficiency of the system and improved the functioning of the NHS is a moot point. Increases in productivity could be explained by the extra funding provided for the NHS at the time of the 1992 general election rather than from the increased spending on management; or it could be a mixture of both.

The changes did serve to increase the administrative costs of providers. Some of this administration had a positive side to it in that it allowed better monitoring of care. Cross-country comparisons of administrative costs between health systems indicate that the UK spends little on the administration of the NHS. This cost advantage is largely owing to the fact that the NHS is funded through central taxation, lowering administrative costs in contrast to insurance-based systems. Thus, costs relative to insurance, such as underwriting costs, advertising expenses, allocation of shareholder profits, approval of hospital admissions, and risk calculation are avoided (Madden 1991: 234).

Equity

The NHS's stated equity goal is to allocate health care services according to need and to ensure access to necessary health care regardless of the ability to pay. However, the government's canvass of health sector issues prior to the 1989 reforms identified several inequities in the health system. There were access problems manifested in long waiting lists, variability between parts of the service and marked regional inequalities resulting in different areas being relatively underfunded or overfunded (Madden 1991: 381).

Rationing resources within the NHS was considered to be an equity issue. Informal rationing occurred throughout the service. Formal rationing techniques, such as queues, priority need classes and eligibility rules should all treat equivalent patients equally. Informal rationing, which subverted the equity aim of these formal techniques, included: dilution of service as physicians treated more patients with shorter consultations, rationing by deterrence and ignorance because of complex eligibility rules, and rationing by 'personal predilection' of the physicians (Higgins and Ruddle 1991: 19).

Particular concern was expressed about the effect of the reforms on geographical equity. The British Medical Association criticized this aspect at the time, saying that the NHS was designed to: 'ensure an even spread of health care services throughout the UK. All patients had a complete range of services available to them within their area and it was rarely necessary for them to travel to other parts of the country for routine treatment. This would no longer be the case, if the Government implemented its plans for a so-called internal market' (Madden 1991: 382). Whitehead (1994: 1286) also warned that the reforms would compromise geographical equity and lead to the fragmentation of the services into many competing units.

Historically, there were regional variations in health services, especially the provision of hospitals. Since the mid-1970s, however, UK governments have tried to improve the geographical equity of hospital and community health services, using a Resource Allocation Working Party (RAWP) formula which sets target allocations for health authorities based on the size, demographic make-up and standardized mortality of their populations (OECD 1992: 117). In 1990, RAWP was replaced by an alternative weighted capitation formula, and in 1994 another review led to a much wider range of health status and social factors being incorporated into the formula to measure the needs of different groups and areas.

Inequities were also experienced by ethnic minority groups. Within the NHS, these expressed themselves in difficulties of access to care and in poor quality treatment. This was partly owing to language and cultural differences as well as to racial discrimination. Problems in the type of care received by ethnic minority patients included: poor or no explanation of conditions and treatments; unnecessary medication or treatment; inadequate examinations; racist slurs; and use of parameters and behavioural models culture-specific to white British people. Initiatives to combat these racial inequities include cultural awareness training, use of interpreters, identifying specific health problems of ethnic minority groups, and commissioning an equal opportunities taskforce (McNaught 1988).

Pre-reform, there were concerns about long waiting times for visits to hospital outpatient clinics, brief and impersonal consultations, and the fact that patients had only a 60 per cent chance of seeing a consultant rather than a junior doctor on a first appointment (OECD 1992). Many GP fundholders specified quality standards for patients in their contracts with hospitals, but this gave rise to concerns about 'two-tier care'. The power of GP fundholders allowed them to assist their patients to jump the queue in getting access to secondary care. However, the government formally stopped such GPs negotiating preferential deals with hospitals.

Matsaganis and Glennerster (1994: 33) noted: 'it has been shown that budget variations between fundholding practices were large in the first year . . . even larger in the second and third years'. This was partly because budgets were set on past referral patterns. Initial reports on GP fundholding showed that, in some regions, 'the uptake of fundholding, attracting associate resources, was strongest among the better resourced practices in more prosperous areas' (Whitehead 1994: 308). While there is limited hard evidence, it is unlikely that fundholding practices did discriminate against high-cost patients. GPs were not personally liable for financial overspending, and for much of the period the budgets of fundholders were based on historical levels of expenditures. Moreover, a stop-loss mechanism existed which set a maximum level of health care expenditure per enrolled patient which was the responsibility of a GP fundholder.

Another aspect of equity concerned the distribution of care and expenditure among different income groups. A study of equity among health care systems found that the UK's was mildly progressive, with the distribution of health care payments almost exactly matching the distribution of pre-tax income (van Doorslaer *et al*. 1993). A 1989 survey of family doctor practices established that the quality of care received by patients from family doctors was linked to patient location and type of practice. Innovative group practices that tended to reward doctors with higher incomes were mainly to be found in more affluent areas.

Choice

British citizens are free to choose their GP and can change GP if they wish; however, there is little choice in rural areas (OECD 1992: 115). Individuals can also opt to purchase over-the-counter medicine from pharmacists, or visit a hospital accident and emergency department. There is limited choice surrounding secondary care since GPs coordinate patients' care and control referrals to hospitals and specialists.

Patients are less informed than doctors in the doctor–patient relationship, and the system has not emphasized education of those users. In the primary care sector, individuals were not encouraged to exercise their right to change practitioner. In the hospital sector prior to the reforms, systems of payment were set up so that 'money did not follow the patient' as care was referred to hospitals from GPs. Hence, patient and doctor choice among different hospitals did not result in high revenues for those hospitals that attracted more patients. Post-reform, there is evidence that some patients were able to choose whether to wait for surgery or travel to another hospital for treatment at an early date (Propper 1995: 79). The reforms also benefited public health by targeting risk factors such as smoking, nutrition and the environment, and by setting clear guidelines for the improvement of health status, the reduction of risk factors and the development of services to improve and protect health (Holland 1994: 187).

The shift to PCGs will draw on a wider range of health care professionals to determine patient needs than did the former GP fundholding schemes. Nevertheless, both approaches have maintained the power of providers in determining access to services on behalf of users. The latest reform further reduces opportunities for individuals and communities to choose a purchaser.

Some commentators have suggested that limited freedom of choice under the Thatcher reforms reflected a trade-off between greater choice and the objectives of cost control and equity (Weale 1988: 69). Since the containment of costs and equity were important principles guiding the direction of the NHS, freedom of choice was correspondingly subordinated. This distinguished the health reforms from reforms in other areas of social policy, where the Conservative government encouraged a more competitive environment and placed purchasing power in the hands of consumers.

It would not be surprising if some groups objected to the role of GPs as 'double agents' and argued for approaches to health care which were more responsive to patients' demands and needs. Constitutional reforms involving greater devolution to Wales and Scotland bring prospects of greater diversity within the system. The reforms have purchased more cost containment and central control over practice, but at the price of less innovation and responsiveness.

Conclusion

While the key policy drivers attached to the Thatcher reforms were choice and competition, it appears that neither goal was achieved to any considerable degree. When competitive forces served to challenge the viability of prestigious London hospitals, the government rushed in to avoid closures and substituted a planned approach, with minimal disruptions to the status quo. The government was unprepared to let market outcomes occur. These actions provided a clear signal that both efficient and inefficient providers were 'safe' within the NHS because the service resisted real market competition. There is merit in the view that competition in the internal market did not fail, because it was never tried (Le Grand 1999) since competitive forces were at best muted. Enthoven has suggested that on a scale of one to ten, the forces of competition within the UK internal market would score between two and three.

The UK experiences with the internal market are remarkable in that such major organizational changes appear to have had very limited impact on policy goals such as equity, efficiency, quality, choice and accountability. From all accounts, the reason appears to be that incentives were relatively weak and constraints were so strong that the market was not able to effect major changes. Yet another impediment to the systematic measuring of impacts was the Conservative government's resistance to undertaking appropriate evaluations of the changes. By contrast, the Labour government appears to be making a more concerted effort to commission evaluative studies to assess the impacts of its reforms.

There seems little doubt among commentators that the Labour government's reforms will lead to greater centralization and control by government, especially as they strengthen the government's authority to cap budgets. Therefore, what appears at first to be substantial gains in provider independence is, at best, a gain that may hold for all providers at the expense of autonomy for specific providers. The importance of clinical independence to GPs means that it is unclear whether any perceived system problems will be linked to the inadequacies of practitioners or, alternatively, to deficiencies in government policies. As was the case with the earlier reforms, providers rather than purchasers are likely to have the upper hand in terms of influencing the shape of events and also, public opinion.

Evidence to date suggests that the fundholding experiments were successful because of innovation, managerial competence and interest, which were stimulated by the reforms. In contrast, the PCGs will require all GPs to participate, not only those who wish to, and will require GPs to share control with a number of other provider groups. From a cost containment viewpoint, these arrangements may appeal, but will require GPs to find ways of controlling the behaviour of their colleagues. When they are coupled with provisions for much longer contracts between purchasers and providers, it appears that some of the individual initiative and innovation which was tapped into through the GP fundholding period will be lost. The difference between the initial design and the implementation of the Thatcher reforms leads one to be somewhat cautious in predicting the final shape and impacts of the proposals. One possibility, however, is that the government has initiated a period of increasing centralization and confrontation with the medical profession over clinical autonomy.

The question arises as to how a balance will be reached between the government's willingness to fund health care and the judgements of medical providers as to what may give value for money. While this is unlikely to be the intention, the relationship of PCGs to their communities could place them in an excellent position from which to draw attention to the inadequacies of public resources. Moreover, if equity is associated with uniformity of approach, PCGs may have reduced scope to respond to the requirements of diverse individuals and community groups, and therefore to achieve gains in technical and allocative efficiency.

NEW ZEALAND

The New Zealand health care system serves 3.8 million people. Health expenditures, both in absolute terms and as a percentage of GDP, are close to the average of OECD countries. Health expenditure was 5.3 per cent of GDP in 1986, rising to 8 per cent in 1998. Funding is derived predominantly from general taxation and there are no explicit social insurance arrangements. Free in-patient treatment was introduced to New Zealand in 1938. By 1947, a predominantly tax-funded health care system was in place, which included government subsidies for GP services. The primary sector in New Zealand includes doctors in general practice and other health providers, who attract partial subsidies (called health benefits) from the government. The main areas of private provision have been general practitioner services and rest home care for the elderly, though both areas receive health benefits. Health benefits provide subsidies for consultations (which are commonly paid directly to the practitioner) and full or partial subsidies on pharmaceuticals, laboratory tests and diagnostic imaging. The government does not regulate the price of primary care, but tries to influences its level via the amount of the subsidy paid. Individuals, through insurance or out-of-pocket payments, meet the balance of funding.

Health benefits are called 'patient subsidies' and GPs have maintained their right to charge a fee-for-service which exceeds the benefit. While initially the part-charge was small, health benefit levels declined over time. Not all people enrol with a general practice, and health policies provide different levels of health benefit to specific groups, such as children, individuals with high demand for services, and those on low incomes. While primary care subsidies continue to be offered on a universal basis, others are targeted. Co-payments on most primary care services (but not hospital services) can encourage the inappropriate use of accident and emergency departments as a source of primary care and provide incentives for individuals to purchase private health insurance.

Although New Zealand's morbidity and mortality patterns are similar to those in other western countries, there are four- to five-year differentials in the levels between Maori (the indigenous people of New Zealand) and non-Maori. The lower health status of Maori can be explained largely by socio-economic and lifestyle factors, which contribute to conditions such as diabetes, cardio-vascular diseases and obesity.

Public and private roles

The public sector's share of total expenditure in 1998/99 was 77.5 per cent: 68.9 per cent from the health vote, 2.9 per cent from other government departments and city councils, and 4.7 per cent from the Accident Rehabilitation and Compensation Insurance Corporation (ARCIC). This no-fault accident and rehabilitation scheme provides access to care and income maintenance in the form of earnings-related compensation. In 1999 legislation was introduced to allow employees to purchase private insurance cover for workplace accidents; however, a change of government shortly thereafter has reinstated the dominance of the public insurer. Private funding comprised private out-of-pocket household spending (15.9 per cent), private insurance (6.2 per cent) and contributions from charitable organizations (0.4 per cent). Spending from vote: health included 60.2 per cent for institutional care, including public (49.0 per cent) and private (11.2 per cent) establishments; and 34.8 per cent to community care.

Private insurers provide supplementary cover and assist individuals to meet patient costs arising from visits to GPs and specialists, as well as charges for elective surgery and medical treatment in private hospitals. Compared with other countries, the private insurance market is relatively undeveloped and unregulated.

Total health care spending as a percentage of GDP has grown little in real terms since the 1980s; however, there have been some noticeable shifts in the sources of funding. In the 1990s there was a downward trend in the share of funding from public sources, and the relative importance of private expenditure increased. Between 1980 and 1998/99 the share of public expenditure dropped from 88.1 per cent to 77.5 per cent, while the share of private sector expenditure grew from 11 per cent to 22.5 per cent. New Zealand's per capita health expenditure in real terms grew over this period at an annual rate of 2.8 per cent; however, private sector spending increased by 6.2 per cent and public expenditure by only 2.1 per cent.

The public sector funds free maternity care and dental care for people under age 16 (age 18, if they are in school). GPs are usually the first point of contact for patients, and act as gatekeepers for hospital and specialist care. In only a few specialities is it common for patients to access specialists directly and without referral. Apart from maternity care, it is uncommon for GPs to operate from public hospitals.

General practitioners supply a range of non-specialist services, and many undertake extra training in order to qualify them to provide maternity care. Public subsidies for birthing have been extended to midwives, and this has resulted in their becoming a major provider of maternity care. General practice services do not provide access to sophisticated technologies, and laboratory tests and other diagnostic services are usually undertaken at laboratories or special facilities. Pharmaceuticals are dispensed from pharmacies, which are usually separate from doctors' surgeries.

The government has responded to shortages of primary care providers by employing staff under special contractual arrangements. Trained medical specialists are recruited from overseas to fill vacancies in public hospitals. While doctors are largely self-regulated, changes are being developed to ensure that medical specialists maintain their levels of competence and undertake work in environments which are safe and suited to the procedures.

Most secondary care is provided by hospitals owned by the government, whereas primary care is funded on a fee-for-service basis and is delivered by self-employed providers. Private hospitals provide outpatient services, elective surgery and long-stay geriatric care, but have limited involvement in areas like mental health, disability and maternity. These patterns are reflected in expenditure trends which showed that in 1996/97, government spending on primary care was predominantly on privately owned GP services, whereas 95 per cent of hospital medical and surgical services were provided by publicly owned providers. In the same year, services for age-related disability support were 38 per cent public and 62 per cent private, while other health and disability support services were 46 per cent public and 54 per cent private.

There is competition between public and private hospitals for patients and medical staff. Private hospitals provide individuals with a choice of specialist and quicker access to elective surgery, while accident and emergency care is undertaken in public hospitals. Many specialist consultants split their time between public and private hospitals, receiving a salary for their public hospital work, but significantly higher fee-for-service payments for work in private hospitals.

Patient access to public hospital acute or chronic care is gained either through accident and emergency facilities or by referral from general practitioners. In the case of public psychiatric hospital care, the Mental Health (Compulsory Assessment and Treatment) Act 1992 defines criteria for the admission and discharge of patients with mental disorders.

Starting in 1983, hospital and community services were organized through 14 area health boards (AHBs), which were allocated funding on the basis of a population-based formula and were responsible for hospital and community health services. Funding for primary care was administered centrally by the Department of Health and provided a system of health benefits which subsidized visits to the GP and also the cost of other inputs, including diagnostic tests and pharmaceuticals. Administration of disability services was managed centrally and responsibilities were split between the Department of Health and the Department of Social Welfare. AHBs were governed by boards, with a mixture of elected and, later, appointed members.

During the mid- to late-1980s, the Labour government commissioned reviews of health benefits and of hospitals. These reviews suggested that the existing system had poor incentives for efficiency arising from the separate funding streams for primary and secondary care, disability services and services for those covered by the accident compensation scheme. Concerns were expressed about the domination of the hospital as provider, arising from the integration of the funding and purchasing roles within the AHBs; AHBs' tendency to overspend and to run down capital investment by deferring maintenance; and their tendency to give low priority to public health care. The reviews considered the possibility of a purchaser–provider split, coupled with new opportunities for competition, on the basis of price but also with regard to new ways of delivering services (Scott *et al.* 1986; Gibbs *et al.* 1988).

Proposals for reform

Following the election of a National government in 1990, a further review of the health system was undertaken, and the government moved decisively to introduce major structural changes to the system. The proposal involved a purchaser–provider split and competition between public and private purchasers and providers. Four government-owned public purchasers of care, called regional health authorities (RHAs), were established to act as regional monopsony public purchasers, replacing the 14 AHBs which both purchased and provided hospital services and delivered public health services. The reforms made provision for the development of private purchasers, called alternative health care plans, which would compete with public purchasers (Upton 1991).

Hospitals were reorganized into 23 Crown Health Enterprises (CHEs). The CHEs were designed to overcome certain weaknesses of the previous area health boards, including poor performance and inadequate accountability and governance arrangements. CHEs were established, many as monopoly providers, in their regions.

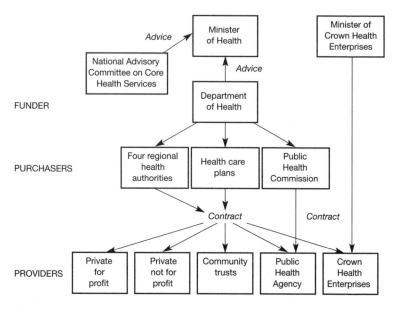

Figure 5.2   New Zealand health sector reform proposals, 1991
Source: based on Upton (1991)

Although it was expected that competitive pressures among them would be increased over time, this did not occur.

A key aspect of the reforms was the integration of public funding across the primary and hospital sectors. There was some targeting of assistance in primary care to high-risk/low-income groups, and part-charges were introduced at the hospital level. The extension of patient co-payments to out-patient and in-patient services in hospitals was unpopular and difficult to sustain, and both features were abolished. Another important goal was to define the nature and limits of public entitlement to core services, and to allow individuals to purchase efficient supplementary insurance. The government defined core services as 'health and disability support services the Government should ensure are purchased, with due respect to its limited means, in order that people have access to effective services on fair terms'. An independent National Advisory Committee was formed with the task of defining core services; being advisory, however, there was no guarantee that the Committee's recommendations would be acceptable or affordable to the government.

The Committee rejected a number of possible approaches to defining a national core, such as a general positive list of core services in the core; a small negative list of services excluded from the core; and a priority-ranked approach, such as that adopted in the state of Oregon. In 1993, the Committee proposed four criteria to determine the circumstances under which services should be publicly funded for an individual: (1) benefit or effectiveness of the service; (2) value for money or cost-effectiveness; (3) fairness in access to and use of the resource; and (4) consistency with the community's values. The baseline or 'implicit core' of services includes broad general areas of primary care, secondary and tertiary medical and surgical services, mental health services and disability support services. It decided to make gradual changes to the implicit core (those services already funded), basing recommendations for change on criteria affirmed by public consultation.

The National government believed that access to a basic package of core health services should not limit opportunities for individuals to access services beyond the core, whether through private insurance or out-of-pocket payments. Thus, the reform contained provisions whereby individuals had the ability to opt out and to transfer their funding entitlement to core services to a private purchaser. The value of this entitlement was to be fixed at an amount which reflected the risk in terms of both the individual's expected need for health care and their income characteristics, so as to ensure affordability and to reduce the tendency of private insurers to cream-skim.

There was early enthusiasm for the reforms from Maori, who were attracted to alternative health care plans as a means to gain greater control over services. However, pooling the risk of Maori into a single health care plan raised concerns that such plans might fail if there were inadequacies in the risk assessment. Although the Health and Disability Services Act 1993 made explicit provision for health care plans (HCPs), the National government announced that it had no immediate intention to establish them.

The government's health reforms followed the design of other economic and social policy changes. The split between the functions of purchaser and provider clarified the separate interests of the government as a purchaser of health care and as the owner of hospitals. CHEs were asked to operate as successful businesses and to seek returns not unlike those obtained by firms in the private sector. These goals were reflected in the appointment of businesspeople to the CHE establishment boards. However, following widespread public concern about these proposals, the legislation was modified. The new legislation required a CHE, while operating as a successful and efficient business, to 'exhibit a sense of social responsibility by having regard to the interest of the community in which [it] operates' (Health and Disability Services Act 1993, section 11). It also allowed CHEs to be directed by ministers, but with the understanding that explicit compensation would be paid for such services.

The reforms gave greater emphasis to population-based strategies for preventing disease, prolonging life and promoting health, including the promotion of healthy lifestyles, ensuring safe food and water, and controlling epidemics. Under the 1993 health reforms a Public Health Commission (PHC) was created as a Crown entity, at arm's length from the government, with a brief to monitor the state of public health, to advise the minister of health on public health, and to purchase or arrange for the purchase of public health services. The PHC purchased services by contracting with providers, including CHEs and other private and public sector agencies.

In July 1995, the PHC was abolished as a separate entity, and its functions and staff were integrated into the Ministry of Health. Responsibility for purchasing shifted to the regional health authorities. While there were several factors which contributed to its demise, the organization clearly fulfilled its brief of promoting public health messages, though at a cost in terms of relationships between the government and certain industry groups.

Implementation of the reforms in 1993 were confounded by political problems which imposed constraints on arrangements surrounding purchasers and providers. Purchasers and CHEs were constrained by requirements to provide the same range and level of services, with the same terms of access, as were available during the previous year. Subsequent to the release of the 1993 Green and White Paper, the four RHAs assumed responsibility for both health and disability support services, though disability expenditures were ring-fenced within the budgets of the RHA. Progress was slower than expected in defining core services, and technical and information problems limited the feasibility of risk-rating individuals (so that they could move to an alternative health care plan). In its 1993 report to the government, the National Advisory Committee on Core Health and Disability Support Services recommended the introduction of a booking system for non-urgent procedures, a policy which has since been adopted.

The new structures were established with various limitations and transitional arrangements governing their operation. For example, decisions by CHEs to expand service capacity were subject to whether or not the government, as owner, considered the investment to be prudent. RHAs agreed to retain fee-for-service payments until December 1995 for general practitioners and private specialists, unless other forms of contracting were adopted. Service entitlements for some disability support consumers were maintained at existing levels until July 1996. Maintaining existing open-ended subsidies for GP services thwarted the efforts of the RHAs to get demand-driven expenditure under control. The need to maintain existing service patterns limited the capacity of the RHAs to demonstrate their ability to become 'smart' purchasers. The three-year parliamentary term resulted in a short timeframe for the implementation of such an ambitious reform agenda. Despite extraordinary efforts by officials, the reform timetables could not be met. The financial position of CHEs proved to be much worse than was envisaged at the commencement of the reforms, and further unanticipated cash injections were required to improve their balance sheets.

Although the creation of the RHAs was designed to establish independent purchasing authorities, politicians continued to exert influence over purchasing decisions. The changes did not increase hospital autonomy, and instead, accountability to the centre was increased. Under the reforms, central government agencies made decisions about RHA pricing policies, CHE capital expenditures and the rationalization of services in sensitive areas. Meetings of the CHEs and RHAs were closed to the public and communities perceived that they had insufficient access to decision-makers.

The reforms brought much greater attention to the government's regulatory policies and drew attention to the need to enforce uniform standards across the public and private sectors. Criticisms were made that public and private sector providers faced different regulatory environments, and that the focus was often on institutions and providers rather than on consumers and the environment in which services were provided. Similar risks received diverse treatment, because they occurred in different settings. The broad thrust of the reforms was to shift its emphasis from providers and institutions towards the safety of consumers.

The need to negotiate a coalition agreement after the 1996 election led to some policy reversals, and further ambiguity regarding the government's long-term vision for the health system. The four RHAs were merged into a single monopsony purchaser at the national level, named (euphemistically) the Health Funding Authority (HFA). CHEs were renamed Hospital and Health Services

(HHS) and given not-for-profit status. Policies were introduced which made GP services and pharmaceuticals free at the point of use for children under 6 years of age. Although the coalition government was subsequently replaced by a National minority government, the free GP visits for children under 6 were retained. The HFA established better information and monitoring systems and approaches for priority-setting within and between services, including quality-adjusted life-years (QALYs) and other measures of cost-effectiveness.

The health reforms have suffered from unclear policy intentions, and although total expenditures in the sector have increased, there is a wide public perception that the government has a strong focus on cost containment. A substantial number of changes were made to organizational arrangements for purchasing and provision between the design and implementation stages of the reforms. A proliferation of agencies for policy development, funding, purchasing and provision led to some confusion about roles and accountability relationships. The establishment of the HFA provided an opportunity to set up clearer accountability frameworks for services purchased and also a more uniform national approach to the pricing of hospital services.

In December 1999, a new centre-left coalition government was elected which announced its intention to make further organizational changes to the health care system. The HFA, the single national purchaser, merged with the Ministry of Health, and some purchasing will be devolved to 22 district health boards (DHBs) whose members will be elected during the latter part of 2001. Arrangements between DHBs and integrated care schemes, GPs and IPAs and Maori providers are being developed as are the roles of and governance arrangements for DHBs. DHBs will combine the roles of regional purchasing and the provision of public hospital care and thus, share some characteristics with area health boards which existed in the 1980s. The government has released a discussion paper concerning a primary care strategy which involves funding of general practice on the basis of capitation. Significant part-charging for primary care will make it difficult to develop managed care schemes based around primary care providers. In addition, however, there is still considerable public resistance to the notion that individuals would be required to enrol with a particular primary care provider.

The reforms reintegrate purchasing and provision of hospital services though some separation has been maintained through the establishment of separate advisory committees for health needs and hospital governance. Although DHBs resemble AHBs, they differ because they will have responsibility for managing agreements with primary, community and Maori providers, although the form of these agreements remains unclear.

System impacts

Public understanding of the rationale and nature of the 1991 reforms was poor, with attention focused primarily on part-charging and on issues surrounding the restructuring of health organizations. Much effort was expended in establishing new structures and contracting arrangements among funders, purchasers and providers of health care, and the deadlines established for implementation could not be met. The decision to roll over elements of funding, purchasing and service delivery was a political and pragmatic response to turbulence and structural change; however, the postponements limited opportunities to alter existing service patterns and improve system performance. Although competitive purchasing did not take place, both cost containment and efficiency were potentially improved by the integration of funding for primary and secondary care. This placed funds under a single public purchaser, which gave the government greater potential to contain costs, and shift resources between primary and secondary care.

Efficiency

The health reform proposals saw competition as an important vehicle for achieving both allocative and technical efficiency. While this was portrayed in the public debate as predominantly price competition, the reforms allowed for competition to occur in a number of dimensions, including service providers, service conditions, quality and technology. In areas like Maori health, the reforms facilitated the development of innovative, local solutions to health problems and further encouraged the growth and development of Maori health providers and providing organizations.

There is little empirical evidence on the impact of the reforms on allocative efficiency; however, a number of policies were introduced which aimed to further this goal. They include: the pooling of funding for primary, secondary and tertiary care with a view to making it easier to shift resources between levels of care within a global budget limit; the introduction of formula which allocates funding to RHAs according to a needs-weighted, population-based formula; the specification of priorities and specific targets for areas such as Maori health and public health; the introduction of evidence-based clinical guidelines for a range of common conditions and services; the introduction of booking systems, based on clinical guidelines for elective surgery; and reference pricing for prescription medicines within therapeutic groups, based on evidence of clinical value and cost-effectiveness. Both the RHAs and the HFA put considerable effort into developing a more rational and transparent process for purchasing services including, in particular, a system for guaranteed maximum waiting times for elective surgery, based on clinical assessment (Scott *et al.* 2000).

While financial difficulties were perceived in the hospitals pre-reform, the reforms made these more apparent. Expectations of quick and substantial increases in efficiency proved to be unrealistic, and problems of performance continued, sometimes resulting in sanctions such as the removal of the chief executive or chair of the CHE. The hospital reforms are difficult to evaluate, both because of data limitations and also the fact that additional funding was put into the system during this period. Lengths of stays in hospital have continued to fall, and the pooling of funding for primary and secondary care under RHAs facilitated the shifting of care from hospital to community settings. There is some evidence of gains in the management and governance areas.

As a measure of improvements in technical efficiency, an estimate of public hospital aggregated output was devised, using a weighted sum of outpatient, day-patient and inpatient volumes. It was estimated that outputs increased at an annual average rate of 0.3 per cent. Increased funding to the sector and changes to the way in which data are collected have made it difficult to obtain reliable measures of changes in output over this period.

The New Zealand reforms demonstrated some of the policy challenges which arise when reforming a health care system that is dominated by public funding, purchasing and provision. There was considerable slippage between the original reform design and that which was implemented. While the government introduced policies which required competition as a vehicle for making efficiency gains, both the public and politicians exerted strong pressure on the system to retain the status quo.

The reforms had an agenda of trying to overcome geographical monopolies; however, CHEs, which were largely regional monopolies, enlisted the support of their communities in thwarting efforts to rationalize services. In addition, their approaches to planning did not inspire confidence that the Crown's ownership interest was being protected. Regional purchasers too found it difficult to alter historical purchasing patterns, and while there were efforts to monitor and steer the sector towards improvements in performance, the energies of the purchasers were centred on the financial aspects of the reforms.

CHEs encountered pressure from purchasers and shareholders to reduce costs; however, staff, politicians and the community put pressure on the system to increase wages and service levels, and to avoid rationalization of service delivery. CHEs provided levels of service outside the boundaries of their contracts and then placed pressure on the purchasers and the government for more money. When CHEs ceased services once they reached their contracted levels, they were, on occasions, directed to provide them, and were restrained from rapidly withdrawing services.

Expectations of financial savings were disappointed as CHE deficits continued to rise. The reasons for the difficulties are many, but contributing factors were the legacy of run-down and over-valued assets. The former AHBs were noted for poor accounting and financial systems, and as these were improved, the poor financial position of the CHEs was more fully revealed. Moreover, no specific provision was made for the costs of implementing reforms, which further contributed to the CHE deficits. The health reforms were effective in establishing a much clearer set of contracting and accountability relationships among funders, purchasers and providers. Following the establishment of the HFA, a standard approach was taken to prices at the national level, thus substituting one uniform national approach for what were 23 separate bilateral negotiations on price. As a result of this work, the efficiency of CHEs was estimated through the use of data envelopment analysis and this resulted in price increases to CHEs. Higher prices and compensation for levels of service in excess of contract requirements acted to eliminate the deficits of ten CHEs.

Data have remained scarce by which to demonstrate the impact of these reforms on the productivity and efficiency of the system. The presence of monopoly and monopsony elements in the service delivery systems served to hinder competitive and efficiency. Poor incentives existed for clinicians to work with managers to reduce costs, and unions extracted early gains from weak CHEs which they used as a lever in negotiations with other CHEs. Efficiency gains were made in some areas, however, such as the contracting-out of domestic services. In addition, major changes to the forms of clinical practice are just beginning to occur, in some cases encouraged by the movement of clinicians into management positions. Some CHEs have exited from residential care for the elderly and community services for mental and disability health clients. It is most unlikely that the shifting of care from institutional to community settings could have been achieved if elected AHBs had still been in place.

The HFA emphasized the targeting of resources to specific groups and conditions at a national level, as well as developing strategies to improve access to primary care services for children and disadvantaged groups. Considerable attention was given to the development of more formal approaches to establishing cost-effectiveness and more robust systems for priority-setting. Considerable progress was made in determining public entitlement and in linking health care outputs to improvements in health outcomes. One example of this was the introduction of a system of guaranteed maximum waiting times for elective surgery based on clinical assessment. Work began on the use of QALYs to measure effectiveness at the margin across health services. In the area of population health, new strategies were utilized to reach those sectors of the population with poor health outcomes. One area of significant improvement was immunization, where rates grew from less than 60 per cent to around 90 per cent over the period 1992 to 1996.

Cost containment

At the time of the reforms, the government decided to focus its primary care subsidies on those with low incomes, to increase user charges for pharmaceuticals and introduce new laboratory, hospital inpatient and outpatient charges. The policies were expected to encourage better use of limited public resources, but were unpopular, and several provisions were removed.

The reforms were introduced with expectations of saving costs by improving contracting arrangements and allowing greater risk-sharing among individuals, purchasers and providers of health care. Purchasers and providers, in particular, were put under pressure by funders to explain why earlier expectations of cost savings and efficiency gains were not achieved.

The more explicit and transparent approach to contracting and rationing services was a phenomenon which the public had not experienced before. Some hospitals threatened to withdraw services once their contracted service levels had been reached, and this led to increased funding for acute care. Unanticipated calls for further funding contributed to an ongoing policy focus on strategies for containing costs.

Substantial cost savings resulted from the establishment by the four RHAs of a jointly owned organization called the Pharmaceutical Management Agency (PHARMAC). It assumes responsibility for determining the pharmaceuticals to be subsidized and negotiated prices with pharmaceutical manufacturing companies. By concentrating purchasing power, PHARMAC was successful in securing substantial savings on pharmaceutical costs and improvements to the efficiency and quality of expenditures.

Equity

The equity goal implicit in the reformed health care system was to provide all citizens with reasonable access to agreed core health services according to their health need. Emphasis was placed on equal access to core services rather than on equal outcomes or expenditure. The strategy was designed to direct the government's limited resources to those with poor health status and limited private resources. Clarification and uniformity of public entitlement were considered to be important ingredients in a fairer system. Knowledge about the nature and limits of state support was also required so that individuals could make informed decisions about the benefits of purchasing supplementary insurance cover.

The reforms raised expectations that the public would become more informed about its public entitlement, and introduction of a booking system for elective surgery can be viewed as a step in this direction. More formal assessment systems also promote equity by ensuring that those most in need and able to benefit were given priority in terms of access to service.

Access to funding for primary care allowed the national and regional purchasers to replace a fee-for-service reimbursement system with more explicit forms of contracts with GPs. New forms of contracting have introduced greater flexibility and innovation in service delivery, and allowed purchasers more scope to offer service coverage in areas which had poor access to practitioners. While contracting for services requires resources, it was a useful device for setting out expectations regarding service conditions and led to improvements in service quality.

Equity entails consideration of socio-economic, locational and cultural dimensions. Cultural barriers and low socio-economic status contribute to the poor access of some Maori to health care. The reform period continued earlier efforts to increase the number of Maori health providers and to tailor services to improve their responsiveness and effectiveness.

Priority-setting is often driven by the goal of greater efficiency in terms of making the best investment to bring marginal benefits in terms of health outcomes. However, marginal dollars can often produce greater health gains for those with higher health status; thus, the identification of target services and populations directs attention to the equity as well as efficiency dimensions of priority-setting. Funding agreements have identified priority areas, including child, Maori, mental and physical environmental health. This approach can be viewed as a way of providing an equity dimension to priority-setting.

Choice

A major goal of the 1993 health reforms was to increase individual choice regarding purchasers and providers, and also clarity regarding core services, and the need for supplementation. The reforms expanded the range of providers of care, particularly at the primary level, thus extending patient choice. They brought important developments in the area of primary care, including the establishment of independent practitioners associations (IPAs). These organizations represented their members in negotiations with the public purchaser, improved management practices and processes and established a better research and information base. Most of the IPAs have participated in budget-holding for laboratory tests, pharmaceuticals and community services, and savings in the range of 8–23 per cent have been observed for some practices (Malcolm 1997). Funds saved by the IPAs can be redirected to health care and related services.

The HFA developed several pilot integrated care experiments, which ranged in scope from improving coordination among providers, to budgetholding by organizations acting as purchasers of comprehensive packages of care. Although proposals did not proceed, the experiments were to evaluate and inform moves towards a more decentralized and devolved approach to purchasing at regional and local levels.

The reforms produce several initiatives targeting better health outcomes for Maori. The more open and competitive contracting environment has encouraged the development of Maori health professionals, the creation of new Maori provider groups and the development of services which were more responsive and appropriate. Greater flexibility in contracting arrangements for care encouraged health professionals to innovate, to work together and to be sensitive to the preferences of those receiving heath care services.

Conclusion

The New Zealand health reforms of the 1990s were ambitious in their design. The short time for implementation of major organizational reform led to unrealistic expectations and an undue focus on institutional change as the vehicle for efficiency gains. Moreover, diverse views regarding the strategic intent and the final aim of the reforms impaired policy coherence and obstructed broad understanding of the reform strategy. Uncertainty remained as to the balance that would be struck between maintaining entitlement to a universal common core and targeting public assistance towards those with the greatest needs.

The proposed introduction of competitive purchasing required clarity and transparency of entitlement; however, it proved difficult to define core services, in part because greater transparency would increase the government's exposure to risk. Contracts and service conditions which were specified too precisely run the risk of locking in technology and stifling innovation and efficiency. On the other hand, a poorly defined core limits efficiency and equity of access, delays any move to competition among purchasers and thwarts the efforts of individuals to buy efficient supplementary care from competing private insurers.

The abolition of area health boards in the early 1990s was driven, in part, by a wish to shift resources and purchasing from secondary to primary care settings. The separation of purchaser and provider assisted that strategy, and was instrumental in fostering greater emphasis on innovation in primary care. The latest round of reforms are being challenged by some Maori and other provider groups which contract on a national basis, and do not wish to negotiate contracts with 21 separate boards. Also, the boundaries of independent practitioner associations are unlikely to conform with those of the district health boards.

The development of the new arrangements is far from complete and it is therefore premature to assess their likely effects. Although the government has indicated its intention to devolve purchasing decisions, major questions arise as to the efficiency of allowing local boards to undertake contracting for some secondary and tertiary care services. In the short term, at least, a recentralization of power is likely, as reflected in the fact that district health board contracts will be vetted first by the Ministry of Health. Disability support services and regional public and mental health services will not be transferred to district health boards until 2002.

6

PUBLIC POLICY
CHOICES

Earlier chapters have analysed public and private roles and interfaces and health reform experiences in seven OECD countries.
Some configurations of public and private roles were shown to be
more effective than others in promoting better health outcomes
and the goals of efficiency, cost containment, equity and choice.
The analysis linked policy choices surrounding roles and interfaces
to perceptions of market and government failure, the determinants
of health outcomes, and the priorities and trade-offs attached to
specific policy goals. This chapter discusses trends, influences and
public policy choices in this area. Whether governments should give
priority to some roles over others is considered, as is the potential
for cross-national learning to inform public policy choices within a
specific country context.

TRENDS AND INFLUENCES

Earlier chapters placed the seven countries into three groups, drawing on common features in terms of system design. Germany and the
Netherlands are universal social insurance systems which allow some
groups to opt out of the public scheme and to purchase private insurance or to self-insure. The United States, Canada and Australia are
federal systems, which result in diverse features across various states
and provinces; they involve a traditional reliance on private insurance and powerful private medical providers. The UK and New
Zealand are both systems reliant on tax-based financing systems,
public hospitals, and the subsidizing of primary care provided by private GPs, who acted as gatekeepers to secondary and specialist care.

While countries within each group shared some common features, there were also important differences. In Germany, for example, patients have direct access to specialists, whereas primary care providers in the Netherlands act as gatekeepers to specialist care. The United States, unlike Canada and Australia, does not provide universal coverage for its citizens. In the UK, but not in New Zealand, patients enrol with a GP, and capitation-based subsidies support GP services. While health system reforms led to GP budget-holding in the UK and integrated care pilots in New Zealand, only UK GP fundholders undertook an active role in purchasing certain secondary care and other services on behalf of their patients.

The seven countries have adopted diverse approaches in terms of the scope of coverage and the interfaces between public and private organizations. In Germany and the Netherlands, both public and private insurers offer comprehensive cover for core services, whereas in the UK and in New Zealand, private insurers offer coverage which is complementary to the public system. In Canada, the interface between private and social insurance arrangements is distinct, and private insurers are prohibited by law from insuring those services which receive public funding and are deemed to be necessary. In Australia, public funding supports the delivery of secondary care in both public and private hospitals.

Health care systems may or may not resemble one another in a number of different dimensions, including policy goals, policy instruments and reform strategies. Despite this, a number of reform trends emerge, including the following:

- *A more important role for private organizations, and greater competition and contestability among public and private funders, purchasers and providers.* Examples include increased competition between public and private providers in the UK and New Zealand; government subsidies in Australia to encourage the purchase of private insurance as an alternative to public insurance; and in the Netherlands, the implementation of policies which are removing the distinctions between public and private insurers in the area of non-catastrophic cover.
- *A more strategic role for governments in overseeing the wider health care system.* A more competitive environment in health care funding, purchasing and provision not only reduced the direct role of government in several countries but also served to increase influence over policy processes, service delivery

arrangements, insurance markets, technological innovations and difficult ethical issues surrounding rationing.

- *Greater attention within reform proposals to the purchasing (or commissioning) role.* Examples include the purchaser–provider split and fundholding arrangements in the UK; the purchaser–provider split, budget-holding and integrated care pilot schemes in New Zealand; and managed care reforms in the United States. The strengthening of the purchasing role has sometimes led to changes in the organization of the purchasing function, but not always. Performance improvements have resulted in several countries from new purchasing strategies in specific areas, such as pharmaceuticals and care for the elderly.
- *Changes to the interfaces between roles.* Reform measures have introduced greater separation of some roles (as in the case of the purchaser–provider split), but also, greater integration of others (for example, managed care and integrated care proposals). Some reforms to health care systems were part of larger public sector reform strategies, which led to clarification and greater competition and contestability in the roles of funding, purchasing, provision, regulation and ownership. Examples include reform proposals in Australia, New Zealand and the UK.
- *Purchasing and providing arrangements with a more integrated view of service delivery.* Policies gave greater attention to outputs and outcomes and less to the subsidization of particular service inputs and provider groups. Service planning approaches concentrated on disease management and the development of comprehensive strategies for prevention and care. Examples include the growth of managed care in the United States, primary and public health reforms in New Zealand and Australia and strategies to improve the coordination of primary, secondary and community care across a number of countries.
- *Continued focus on fiscal problems and strategies involving cost-shifting, risk-sharing and cost containment.* Although some reforms brought increases in funding levels, this was not always anticipated or welcomed.
- *Increased priority was given to improving health outcomes and to demonstrating correlation between health care outputs and better health outcomes.* In making resource allocation decisions, policy-makers placed greater emphasis on information and research, evidence-based medicine, utilization review and processes for priority-setting and rationing, based on the ability to benefit.

- *Reform strategies gave greater emphasis on primary and public health care strategies which link individuals, populations and communities.* Governments implemented promotion, protection and prevention strategies, and policies aimed at reducing health and social risks by altering lifestyle choices. Health strategies were linked to wider social development strategies and encouraged individuals and communities to take greater responsibility for health outcomes.
- *Obstacles to implementing 'big bang' reforms as planned.* Reforms faced opposition from purchasers and users of services, health professionals and a variety of other interest groups. Staff working in public health sector organizations became reorganized and refocused, and many policy-makers suffered 'reform fatigue'.
- *Too much emphasis was placed on structural reform and insufficient attention was given to issues of organizational development and culture.* Reforms of the role of public and private organizations were portrayed as ends in themselves, rather than as a means to better system performance. Some political parties regarded competition and managed care as goals in their own right. Some governments were unable to communicate a clear vision to the public regarding the rationale and likely impacts of their proposed changes. Policy changes were debated in terms of competing ideologies, with limited understanding of the potential for market and quasi-market reforms to improve system performance.
- *Too much optimism on the part of both politicians and public servants concerning the costs of major reorganization and the time required for new systems to deliver benefits.* When governments changed, some chose to distinguish their policies by engaging in further structural change. Others maintained existing organizations but modified goals, objectives, priorities and the language used to describe the reforms.
- *Focus on the degree of choice which individuals enjoy within a health care system and on who should act as the agent for users and consumers.* Some reforms shifted the balance of power away from medical providers and health care institutions and provided individuals with greater choice (in the form of primary care provider, care manager or insurer). Others acted to reduce choice, for example moves to managed care in the United States.

LEARNING FROM INTERNATIONAL EXPERIENCES

Many countries were proactive in seeking information on the system design and reform experiences of other countries. Sometimes lessons were drawn from countries with similar system features, but not always. For example, the 1993 New Zealand proposals for competing health care plans (which were never implemented) drew more inspiration from the Netherlands reforms, involving competition between public and private purchasers and providers, than from the UK reforms. Despite proximity and similar system features, the Netherlands and Germany were less likely to draw lessons from one another than from countries further afield. There is evidence of cross-national borrowing of reforms – or at least relabelling of reform proposals – in order to obtain beneficial results putatively achieved elsewhere (Altenstetter and Bjorkman 1997: 1).

Some have suggested that the comparative policy literature has been too quick to discover convergence (Jacobs 1998). Opportunities for learning can be impaired when policy-watchers do not give sufficient attention to the similarities and differences between reform proposals. For example, the term managed (or integrated) care can take on many different meanings, describing different strategies when used in different country contexts. In systems dominated by public funding and provision, the term 'managed care' may describe strategies for improved coordination across public service providers, with a view to delivering a more seamless service. On the other hand, managed care in the US health care system describes health care insurers, providers and care plans which fund, purchase and provide health care in ways which limit a patient's free choice of provider and treatment.

The term 'managed (or regulated) competition' also assumes different interpretations within different country contexts. In the United States, the focus of managed competition is on price competition between for-profit and not-for-profit firms, while in Germany, competition occurs primarily in dimensions other than price. These differences have led to lively debate among health policy experts as to whether it is even appropriate to use the term 'managed competition' to describe Germany's approach to health sector reform (see Reinhardt 1999). Caution must be exercised when comparing reforms involving internal public sector markets with proposals involving competition among public and private sector organizations.

Reform strategies in different countries have reflected different interpretations, priorities and trade-offs across policy goals. The goal of equity in health care may refer to equal inputs, access to services, utilization of services, or health outcomes. If equity means 'equal access', then resources should provide uniform services for equivalent need, but if defined as 'equal outcomes', then resources should be aimed at those with poor health status. Health systems with substantial elements of public funding are likely to associate equity with the delivery of a uniform service to individuals with similar needs. In contrast, health systems with substantial private funding from individuals and employers are likely to regard the situation as fair in which individuals and employers are able to determine the level of insurance cover and to supplement coverage.

Trade-offs may occur between equity and efficiency because it is often more cost-effective to deliver marginal health gains to those with good rather than poor health status. Governments may promote cost-shifting and cost-containment strategies, even when these result in efficiency losses to the total system. Trade-offs between cost containment and equity were exhibited in Canada in the late 1990s, when cuts to federal spending and greater reliance on provincial funding reduced the capacity of the system to promote greater equity across provinces with respect to need and ability to pay. Systems with a substantial element of private insurance promote greater choice for individuals and employers but compromise equity, if it is defined as equal access for equal need.

Sometimes, cross-national learning is hindered by a tendency in health policy literature to compare policy alternatives in terms of false dichotomies. Welfare states are portrayed as supplanting or suppressing the market, yielding the alternatives of state or market, private or public, competition or cooperation, as the basis of policy choice. As noted in a study on realignments in the welfare state:

> State versus market, strong state versus weak state, regulation versus competition may all have been analytically useful polarities in the early development of welfare states, but the complexities of contemporary social organization invalidate such single-dimensional views of institutional processes and forms. (Ruggie 1996: 259)

Real-world reforms are producing patterns of public and private organizations which defy simple approaches to system classification.

This suggests the need for new typologies to depict health care systems in a way that portrays the complexity of public and private roles and interfaces in the areas of funding, purchasing, provision, regulation and ownership. Policy analysts often face time and information constraints, particularly when policies are changing rapidly. Pressure encourages organizations to defer research efforts and to focus energies on providing information and analysis to feed the ongoing policy process. Analysts should seek reform lessons which are evidence-based, while being aware of constraints on analysis in real-world public policy environments. Constraints exist because it is often difficult to construct controlled experiments which allow causal links between changes to system design and improved system performance. Nevertheless the rapid pace of change to systems provides opportunities to study natural experiments within environments in which some policy settings are changing while others remain constant.

Despite these limitations, policy-makers should be careful not to underestimate the capacity of comparative studies to inform public policy decisions within a specific country. Cross-national learning can provide insights into the relationship between health system design and system performance. Drawing on international experience can potentially provide useful prompts and ideas from which to develop and analyse local policy options. Valuable learning can be derived not only from countries which share common or similar institutional arrangements and design features, but also from those with different system features. In many countries, greater attention should be given to evaluating the impacts of changes to health care systems on health outcomes and health policy goals.

CHOOSING ROLES AND INTERFACES

Policy choices among roles and interfaces are shaped by many different factors. Drawing on previous experiences and trends, we review public policy choices with respect to funding, purchasing and provision. Though policy choices reflect many influences, they appear to be sensitive to individual, community and governmental views on the following matters:

- The presence and magnitude of different sources of market and government failure.
- The nature of health and the influence of health care and other socio-economic determinants on health outcomes.

- The interpretation, priority and trade-offs attached to specific policy goals.

Funding choices

Key public policy choices are whether public funding is to be universal or selective, and the degree to which public funding levels will be modified to respond to differences across population groups and geographical areas. Private insurance is often more specific with regard to the scope and nature of coverage, and commonly defines particular kinds of health service, provider and health care organization. In tax-funded universal systems, access may remain implicit, and information about entitlements is discovered in the course of seeking treatment. Systems which are predominantly tax-funded can offer more uniform access to care than employer-based private insurance systems. Social insurance systems which are organized by occupational class or by provincial area and region produce greater diversity in terms of funding levels and access than do tax-financed systems.

Funding policy choices will reflect views regarding the nature and determinants of health and the relative effectiveness of personal and population-based health interventions. If health is considered to be largely a private good with few externalities, then individual preferences regarding risk and affordability will be given considerable weight in making health care choices about the nature of personal health care services. When public interests override private interests, then public expenditures will be used to pursue public health strategies that are linked to socio-economic and environmental factors in the community. Where the policy focus is on improvements in health outcomes rather than health outputs, then strategies for health gain should focus on interventions other than health care.

Universal coverage overcomes problems of affordability and is effective in redistributing resources among groups. It provides scope for the government to influence the nature of services provided and to ensure that ability to benefit rather than ability to pay is the key criterion governing access.

When governments have a substantial funding role, they can use monopsony powers to exert pressure on prices, volumes and therefore expenditure levels. A concentration of funding sources provides greater potential to achieve total system cost containment and to make choices and trade-offs among different expenditure categories. Where a government regulates price, quality and service conditions, cost containment may be effective even when there are many funders and purchasers. While Canada exerts market influence by means of its 'single funding pipe', Germany's 'many funding pipes' also exert control over expenditure, through government regulations on the volumes and prices of services. Where both public and private funders compete to provide comprehensive cover, then definitions of core services must be more explicit. Although open enrolment and community rating may be introduced to reduce the cost and increase the affordability of insurance cover for higher risk groups, these regulations provide incentives for insurers to engage in cream-skimming. Policy responses, such as explicit compensation to insurers for high-risk groups and reinsurance (to spread the risk), have the potential to reduce, but not eliminate, the tendencies of insurers to cream-skim.

Public policy choices surrounding funding are affected by the priority and trade-offs attached to specific policy goals. In particular, the larger the share of public funding, the greater the government's potential to undertake system-wide strategic public policy interventions. A focus on equity will tend to support a significant public funding role, while emphasis on choice will place greater emphasis on private funding. Allocative efficiency requires that the marginal health gain per dollar is equalized over all categories of expenditure, while technical efficiency requires that outputs of a given quality are produced at least cost. The relationships between public and private funding and technical and allocative efficiency are more complex and relate to views surrounding the nature of health outputs and outcomes, and the presence of different sources of market failure and government failure. Government failure arises from problems related to bureaucratic supply, fiscal externalities and because public decision-making does not yield a level and mix of health care expenditures which maximizes health outcomes. One impediment to getting better resource allocation is the tendency of public bodies to ring-fence budgets according to type of service and level of care. When health care resources are combined within a single global budget, there is greater potential to shift resources across and within services.

Purchasing choices

Reforms affecting the purchasing role have been popular with governments seeking more control over expenditure levels, and the scope and nature of health care which is provided. Public policy choices surrounding purchasing relate to the roles of public and private purchasers and the degree to which private purchasing will be complementary or competitive. Systems dominated by public purchasing are often monolithic in their approach to health care interventions, and may perform poorly against the criteria of efficiency and choice. Purchasing choices relate to risk-sharing and accountability arrangements, and also to the degree to which purchasing should be decentralized or devolved. These choices have implications for the role of individuals, employers, public and private funders, purchasers and providers in determining the nature of services purchased and the criteria for access to care. The relative merits of a single monopsony purchaser and competing purchasers is an area where there is still substantial policy disagreement. Sometimes, competition among purchasers is opposed on the grounds that it results in high transaction costs, market failures (arising from moral hazard and adverse selection), cream-skimming and associated efficiency losses. Yet competitive purchasing is supported on the grounds that it provides much better information to consumers regarding the benefits arising from the purchaser. This view recognizes that higher administrative costs can be justified when they deliver improvements in both technical and allocative efficiency.

Key public policy choices in purchasing concern the size and nature of any set of core services and the degree to which the public entitlement is explicit. An impediment to the introduction of competitive purchasing is the difficulty of getting reliable data to allow the risk-rating of individuals and groups. Estimates of health risk are often difficult to obtain and measures which do not take account of service utilization are poor predictors of risks to funders and purchasers (Hamilton, in Jérôme-Forget *et al.* 1995). In this environment, purchasers will be risk-averse and prefer to compete on the basis of cream-skimming and risk selection rather than on price.

A universal and well defined core provides uniform coverage on the basis of 'one size fits all'; however, the need for services to be appropriate and responsive to diverse groups and cultures suggests that benefits may arise from tailoring packages to be more responsive to the priorities and health risks of particular individuals and groups. Moreover, the influence of lifestyle choices on health status means that successful outcomes are more likely to be achieved when individuals and groups take greater responsibility for their health by directly participating in health care strategies and purchasing decisions. Developing services responsive to the needs of

specific ethnic and cultural groups is likely to improve health outcomes, as is the more active participation of individuals and communities in the development of health strategies. The nature and
variability of health risks and service preferences across groups will
affect the magnitude of benefits to be derived from a more devolved system for purchasing, including choices by individuals of
purchasing agent. Often, there is a need to balance the goal of
maintaining national standards with the benefits of allowing for
differences in local or regional needs and priorities. In some cases,
however, communities of interest will not conform with geographical boundaries, and this will undermine the effectiveness of strategies involving devolution and decentralization.

Providing choices

Policy choices surrounding provision concern the scope and role of
providers and whether there should be competition and contestability among providers. A feature of policy reforms in a number of
countries has been the clarification and, in some cases, organizational separation of the purchasing and provider roles. Both the
UK and New Zealand made this the centrepiece of their reforms
throughout the 1990s, and yet, recent proposals in both countries
call for some reintegration of the two roles. In both countries, the
purchaser–provider split fostered innovation and assisted services
to shift from hospital and institutional settings to primary care and
community settings.

The purchaser–provider split is popular in systems dominated by
public purchasing and provision, since it encourages competition
among public and private providers and allows governments to give
separate consideration to its interests in purchasing and in the
ownership and delivery of health care services. The merits of a purchaser–provider split cannot be divorced from whether there will
be one or many purchasing organizations, the degree to which purchasing will be devolved and the extent of competition among providers. So long as there is risk-sharing, problems surrounding
cream-skimming and the underservicing of patients will arise, even
when there are monopsony purchasing and competing providers.
The health policy challenge is to find ways to manage the risks of
cream-skimming rather than hoping to remove them altogether.

Fundholding and budget-holding experiences in the UK and
New Zealand encouraged greater attention to the cost-effectiveness of treatments at the primary care level. In the UK, these

reforms strengthened the links between primary and secondary care through GP fundholding arrangements; like New Zealand's innovations in the integrated care pilots, primary care schemes and Maori health initiatives, they demonstrated the benefits which can be derived from the integration of purchasing and provision. When there is no competition and contestability among public and private purchasers and providers, the system is unlikely to foster innovation and responsiveness.

The trend in many countries has been to increase the contestability of service provision, particularly in areas where output and quality are easy to measure. Public policy choices in the area of provision can be usefully divided into low-cost, frequently-used services and high-cost, infrequently-used services. Low-cost, frequently-used services are likely to generate efficiency gains if provided competitively, and choice of service allows users to provide better signals regarding quality and the potential for benefit. The trend in many countries has been to increase the contestability of service provision, particularly in the areas where output and quality are easy to measure. High-cost, infrequently-used services may result in asymmetries of information and also monopoly elements which support direct provision and/or the regulation of private providers. Monopoly public supply limits competition on the basis of price, quality, and technology surrounding the service, thus reducing the potential for innovation and efficiency.

Although monopoly public provision is sometimes justified on grounds of market failure, or in terms of benefits arising from economies of scale and scope, the theory of government failure warns of problems arising from bureaucratic supply. Governments which are dominant providers of hospital services possess an important vehicle for controlling not only health system costs but also the introduction of technology.

Despite much discussion in the health policy literature about competitive markets, health care systems which involve a strong public sector presence in the areas of purchasing and provision do not resemble perfectly competitive markets. The outcomes of markets in which there are few buyers and sellers are difficult to predict, and will reflect the relative power of the two groups.

Introducing greater contestability in health service delivery systems can foster greater technical and allocative efficiency. At the same time, governments may remove management and ownership responsibility to arm's-length with a view to containing costs or shifting costs to the private sector. Concerns remain in many countries that for-profit providers of services will encourage service levels to rise and raise public expectations regarding the standard of service delivery. While some governments have placed their focus on curtailing the introduction of high-cost technologies, pressure on expenditures can also result from universal access to low-cost technologies.

Efficiency gains arising from contracting out and greater competition and contestability among services and service providers are easiest to achieve when it is possible to define the nature of the service, quality characteristics and the relationship between outputs and outcomes. Fostering competition has stimulated innovation in service design and delivery, and supported policies which shift care from institutional to community settings. Significant cost savings and improvements in quality have been achieved in categories such as mental health, disability support and services for the elderly. Where services are expensive and difficult to define and contract, public provision may be retained, whether it be to achieve economies of scale or scope, to control the introduction of new technology or to retain oversight of and influence over system costs.

Estimates vary, but it is widely acknowledged that the efficiency and cost-effectiveness of many health care interventions has not been established. Moreover, the effectiveness of health care is person-specific and perceived benefits from care vary when judgements are made by individuals as opposed to health practitioners and professionals. A major challenge for governments is to improve access to care and health outcomes in a way which does not thwart innovation and experimentation in the provision of health care.

CONCLUSION

Reform experience demonstrates that while some configurations of private roles and interfaces are clearly superior to others in terms of supporting particular policy goals, no ideal set of public–private roles and interfaces emerges as international best practice for all countries. The degree of public and private participation in funding, purchasing and provision should be related to the specific country context, policy goals and priorities and to economic, social, cultural and other factors. Our examination of health care systems demonstrates that the health sector can be distinguished from many other sectors of the economy. While its characteristics are not unique, the prominent role of governments in health care reflects, in particular, various sources of market failure in the markets for health care and health insurance. Public intervention is the norm rather than the exception, and the question arises as to whether governments should give priority to some roles over others.

The evidence confirms that governments should maintain a role in funding in order to address market failures in the areas of health insurance and health care, including the existence of public goods, externalities and problems surrounding the income distribution. Public funding is particularly critical for low-income, high-risk groups, and also to capture and internalize benefits and externalities to third parties. The case for government funding is strong in instances when governments wish to finance (and sometimes provide) public goods, especially population-based public health interventions. The size and relative importance of public and private health risks should be a critical factor in determining the scope and volume of the public role in funding. Substantial public health risks require public action, while relatively confined, low-cost private health risks are more amenable to solution by private action.

International experience shows that countries with a substantial funding role have been more successful at cost containment than those which place extensive reliance on private insurance markets. The government's role in purchasing is important too, particularly if public financing is involved. If a set of core services can be defined appropriately, then competition between public and private purchasers is a viable policy option. Defining public and private interfaces within and between functions benefits from clarity regarding not only the nature of the publicly financed core but also the degree to which private insurers and providers are free to fund, purchase and provide core and non-core services. Core services which are too prescribed will reduce incentives for innovation and efficiency. Although governments may in principle support the desirability of providing citizens with greater transparency regarding service coverage, they avoid definitions of entitlement which will lead to open-ended commitments and high levels of risk.

Key choices concern how purchasing will be done and whether individuals will have some choice or voice in these arrangements. The merits of alternative purchasing arrangements will depend upon the nature and variability of health risks and also reflect public expectations and preferences regarding health care. The greater the diversity within the population in terms of economic, social, cultural, geographical and environmental factors, the more likely that health care systems will be designed to respond to the different needs and preferences of citizens, groups and other communities of interest. Public systems are less able to be responsive to individual tastes and preferences, and this is particularly so when purchasing and provision roles are combined. Competition and contestability in purchasing offer greater scope to respond to diverse preferences. Sometimes, the introduction of competition and contestability in purchasing and/or delivery is opposed on the grounds that such systems incur higher administrative costs. While this may be true, health systems must be judged in terms of their capacity to deliver greater efficiency and improved health outcomes, not in terms of minimizing administrative costs.

The case for government provision is weaker than that for funding and purchasing. Many health care systems are subject to monopoly elements, and governments may bring about welfare gains by bargaining with monopoly providers. There is a case for encouraging competition and contestability for services where service costs are relatively low, outputs can be clearly defined and judgements about quality can be made by those who receive the service.

Considerations surrounding market failure and government failure will influence decisions about the role of government in service delivery as well as in the area of regulation. Economies of scale and scope are sometimes used to justify public hospital provision although the potential for government failure is strong where there is monopoly public supply. Most strategies for overcoming substantial government failure in these areas will involve making provision more competitive and contestable. While competition in service delivery may be related to price, it also relates to service conditions, quality dimensions and the attributes of service providers.

Increasing competitiveness in service delivery raises the issue of how the government or other funders and purchasers should subsidize health care services. In some systems, subsidies are attached to particular provider groups, so efforts to increase competitiveness will involve extending the subsidy to new providers. A recent trend is for countries to shift subsidies from particular providers and provider inputs toward subsidizing entire services. This approach encourages both competition and collaboration among different provider groups, while also fostering innovation in service delivery. Policies are to be encouraged which foster a more integrated approach to service delivery, involving strategies for disease management which span different levels of care and encompass preventative as well as curative services.

A key policy choice concerns whether the degree to which individuals should have discretion over their primary care provider, purchaser or health care plan. There are strong reasons for offering individuals a choice of primary care provider and managed care plan, since doing so encourages individuals to take greater responsibility for their health care and promotes better health care outcomes. Benefits from tailoring health packages are greatest in the area of personal rather than public health care. Adopting a population focus requires analysis of the merits and demerits of various policy interventions to determine which are most cost-effective in improving health outcomes.

Publicly financed and delivered health care systems differ from private health care systems because governments make collective financing and purchasing decisions on behalf of the population. Public choices inevitably result in decisions being made which are less responsive to individual tastes and preferences. Public budgets are constrained and rationing is often by queues rather than by prices, as occurs in private markets. Whatever the size and scope of the governmental role, there will be some individuals who will wish to purchase supplementary private insurance or private care.

Recognizing that competitive environments can sometimes reduce the scope for information-sharing, a government should support the production and dissemination of information on the activities and performance of public and private funders, purchasers and providers and on health outcomes. Governments should ensure that there is adequate investment in health sector research and development and that results are shared with the public and with health care organizations.

Governments should maintain strategic oversight over the health care system in areas such as consumer protection, service delivery and quality assurance. While monitoring and evaluation systems can place their focus on inputs, process, outputs and outcomes, the most rewarding investments will be those that measure the impacts of health outputs on health outcomes. Greater attention should be placed on evaluating the impacts of health reforms on system performance. Governments should seek management improvements which encourage greater accountability, transparency and efficiency, but these gains must deliver improvements in system performance. In short, policy-makers should view organizational choices regarding public and private roles and interfaces not as ends in themselves but as part of strategies for seeking better health outcomes and performance improvements in relation to specific policy goals.

As governments shift their focus from service delivery to a governance and leadership role, public policies should monitor and evaluate the performance of both public and private organizations and maintain strategic and regulatory oversight of the health care system. These changes offer the potential for governments to focus on specific policy goals and trade-offs and to redirect resources towards investments which are most likely to improve health outcomes. In this environment, successful public policy will require governments to align the roles, interfaces and behaviours of both private and public organizations.

GLOSSARY

Accountability: The state or position of being accountable; responsibility for actions and decisions; answerability.

Actuarial insurance: Insurance premiums where the expected pay-outs meet the premiums paid by those who are insured.

Adverse selection: The problem encountered in insurance whereby individuals who seek insurance are likely to have higher risk profiles than the population as a whole.

Allocative efficiency: A situation where the level and mix of health care services purchased has maximized health benefits from a particular level of expenditure. This is achieved when the additional benefit for the last pound spent on different services is the same, and equal to the marginal cost of providing the service.

Capitation: A method for funding health care services, including the reimbursement of providers, that pays a fixed amount per person, and is not linked explicitly to the level of service provided.

Case-mix funding: Adjustments to the funding of services providing for differences in patient diagnoses and sometimes for the severity of the illness.

Co-insurance: The share of the cost which is paid by the individual who is insured. In a health plan with 15 per cent co-insurance the individual pays 15 per cent and the insurance company pays 85 per cent of total treatment costs.

Community rating: An insurance programme which charges each member in a region the same premium for a particular level of coverage regardless of the risk profile of any particular individual.

Competitive market: A market in which a very large number of small buyers and sellers trade independently and, as such, have limited influence over market price.

Contestable market: A market in which there is no restriction on entry and exit for suppliers.

Co-payment: Fees that the patient must pay for a medical service, which is designed to discourage overutilization and must usually be paid out of pocket.

Cost-shifting: Actions undertaken by funders, purchasers or providers to shift costs to other organizations or individuals.

Cream-skimming: Behaviour by insurers and those who fund health care to identify and offer insurance to low-risk individuals.

Deductible: An amount that an insured individual must pay prior to the insurance company meeting a claim.

DRG-type prospective payment system: A system for reimbursing providers in which a fixed fee is paid prospectively. The fee is determined by the classification of the medical condition into a diagnosis related group (DRG) rather than by the cost of services delivered.

Equity: Fairness and justice as reflected in some assignment of resources across groups.

Externalities: Benefits or costs arising from the consumption or production of a good or service which extend to third parties.

Experience rating: The setting of insurance premiums with regard to the likely costs of individuals or groups, based on previous claims experiences.

Funder: A public or private organization that provides financing of health care services.

Gatekeeping: The management by a primary care provider of access by patients to specialists and other types of health care.

Government failure: Undesirable consequences of government intervention to overcome problems of market failure.

Health care: Goods and services which are used with a view to improving or maintaining health status.

Inverse care law: A law which suggests that individuals with substantial requirements for health care are likely to have limited ability to pay.

Managed care: Any payment or delivery arrangement used by a health plan or provider to coordinate use of health services with a view to controlling health expenditures, improving quality, or both.

Managed competition: A policy of increased reliance on competing funders or purchasers, involving the organization and delivery of a basic benefits package or set of core services.

Market failure: Circumstances which may provide grounds for government intervention in health care funding and delivery arrangements. They include moral hazard and adverse selection, information asymmetries, monopoly elements and problems of access arising from the distribution of income.

Medicaid: An insurance programme established by the US federal government for low-income beneficiaries which provides minimum standards of care.

Medicare: Public universal insurance schemes in Australia and in Canada that provide access to ambulatory and hospital care. Also, the United States' federal health insurance programme for the elderly and other selected groups.

Monopolist: A supplier which is able to charge above market prices owing to its singular predominance in the market.

Monopsonist: Strictly speaking, a single buyer, but used to describe circumstances where government or private funders and purchasers are making very large purchases and can therefore exert considerable influence on the price of health care services.

Moral hazard: A circumstance where changes in behaviour arise as a consequence of being insured.

Private insurance: Insurance schemes provided in the private sector to cover medical expenses.

Provider: A health professional or organization that is involved in the delivery of health care services.

Purchaser: An individual or organization that makes arrangements for health care to be accessed or purchased.

Purchaser–provider split: A health reform strategy in which a public organization which both purchases and provides services is reorganized so as to separate the two roles. The separation is undertaken with a view to enhancing the competition and contestability of health services provision and sometimes purchasing.

Regulator: Often a central agency or organization that specifies various requirements which must be met as a condition of funding, purchasing or providing health care.

Reimbursement: The process of paying for the costs incurred, especially through a third party.

Risk aversion: A tendency by insurers to be unwilling to insure high-risk groups, leading to an expectation of higher than normal returns as compensation for assuming higher risk levels.

Risk-pooling: The formation of a group to allow individual risks to be spread and shared among many people.

Social insurance: Government or non-profit insurance programmes in which premiums or contributions are subsidized and there is a significant redistribution from some segments of the population to others.

Technical efficiency: A situation when health care outputs of a given quality are produced at least cost.

BIBLIOGRAPHY

Aaron, H. and Schwartz, W. (1984). *The Painful Prescription: Rationing Health Care.* Washington, DC: Brookings Institution.

Aaron, H.J., Bosworth, B., Barry, P., David, M. and Pauly, M.V. (1994). Economic issues in reform of health care financing, *Brookings Papers on Economic Activity: Microeconomics*: 249–99.

Abraham, B., d'Espaignet, E. and Stevenson, C. (1995). *Australian Health Trends.* Canberra: AIHW.

Aday, L.A., Begley, C.E., Lairson, D.R. and Slater, C.H. (1993). *Evaluating the Medical Care System.* Michigan: Health Administration Press.

AIHW (Australian Institute of Health and Welfare) (1996). *Australia's Health 1996.* Canberra: AIHW.

AIHW (Australian Institute of Health and Welfare) (1998). *Australia's Health 1998.* Canberra: AIHW.

Altensetter, C. and Bjorkman, J.W. (1997). *Health Policy Reform: National Variations and Globalization.* New York: St Martin's Press & London: Macmillan Press.

Anderson, G.F. and Poullier, J-P. (1999). Health spending, access, and outcome: trends in industrial countries, *Health Affairs*, 18(3): 178–91.

Appleby, J. (1992*). Financing Health Care in the 1990s.* Buckingham: Open University Press.

Ashton, T. (1999). The health reforms: to market and back?, in J. Boston, P. Dalziel and S. St John (eds) *Redesigning the Welfare State in New Zealand.* Auckland: Oxford University Press.

Baily, M. and Garber, M. (1997). Health care productivity, *Brookings Papers on Economic Activity*, 143–202.

Barer, M.L. and Evans, R.G. (1992). Interpreting Canada: models, mind-sets, and myths, *Health Affairs*, 11: 44–61.

Barer, M.L., Evans, R.G. and Labelle, R.J. (1988). Fee controls as cost control: tales from the frozen north, *The Milbank Quarterly*, 66(1): 1–47.

Barr, N. (1990). *Economic Theory and the Welfare State: A Survey and*

Reinterpretation, discussion paper WSP/54. London: Welfare State Programme, Suntory–Toyota International Centre for Economics and Related Disciplines, London School of Economics.

Behrens, J. (1997). *Freedom of Choice and Quality Assurance – The Social Economic and Organisational Sociology of Freedom of Choice and Market Forces within the Health System*. Conference organized by the Centre for Social Policy Research (ZeD) at the University of Bremen, Germany, 11–12 May.

Bell, A. (1998a). Medigap sales could gain from HMS's retreat, *National Underwriter*, 19 October, 43–5.

Bell, A. (1998b). Rules trip up Medicare recipients, *National Underwriter*, 16 November, 64.

Bennett, A. and Adams, O. (eds) (1993). *Looking North for Health*. San Francisco: Jossey-Bass.

Blendon, R.J. and Blomqvist, Å. (1991). The doctor as double agent: information asymmetry, health insurance, and medical care, *Journal of Health Economics*, 10: 411–32.

Blendon, R.J., Schoen, C., Davis, K. and Binns, K. (1999). The cost of health system change: public discontent in five nations, *Health Affairs*, 18: 206–16.

Bloom, A. (2000). *Health Reform in Australia and New Zealand*. Melbourne: Oxford University Press.

Boothe, P. and Johnston, B. (1993). Stealing the emperor's clothes: deficit offloading and national standards in health care, *C.D. Howe Institute Commentary*, 41: 1–11.

Boston, J., Dalziel, P. and St John, S. (1999). *Redesigning the Welfare State in New Zealand*. Auckland: Oxford University Press.

Brown, R.B., McCartney, S. and Bell, L. (1995). Why the NHS should abandon the search for the universal outcome measure, *Health Care Analysis*, 3: 191–5.

Burchardt, T. (1997). *Boundaries Between Public and Private Welfare: A Typology and Map of Services*. London: Centre for Analysis of Social Exclusion, London School of Economics.

Burton, L. (1996). The ethical dilemmas of the Oregon health plan (health care rationing), *The Nurse Practitioner*, 21(2): 62–7.

Butler, J.R.G. and Doessel, D.P. (eds) (1989). *Health Economics: Australian Readings*. Sydney: Australian Professional Publications.

Butler, P. (1995). Government under fire over London hospital closures, *Health Services Journal*, 9 March: 7.

Calnan, M., Cant, S. and Gabe, J. (1993). *Going Private: Why People Pay for their Health Care*. Buckingham: Open University Press.

Carse, S. (1993). *West German Health Care System Report*. Paper for Advance Public Policy, 402.

Castles, F. (1999). *Comparative Public Policy*, Gloucestershire: Edward Elgar Publishing.

Chadda, D. (1995a). Fundholders account for most emergency referrals, *Health Services Journal*, 30 March: 5.

Chadda, D. (1995b). Fundholding framework is confused, claims IHSM, *Health Services Journal*, 30 March: 8.

Chadda, D. (1995c). One in four fundholders underspent by £100,000, *Health Services Journal*, 2 March: 8.

Chapman, A.R. (ed.) (1994). *Health Care Reform: A Human Rights Approach*. Washington, DC: Georgetown University Press.

Commonwealth Department of Health and Aged Care (1999). *Synopsis of the Reports of the General Practice Reviews*. Canberra: Commonwealth Department of Health and Aged Care.

Cox, J.W. (1998). Health-care coverage gets a chill, *South Florida Business Journal*, 19: 1–2.

Crail, M. (1995). All above board, *Health Services Journal*, 9 March: 11.

Crampton, P. and Howden-Chapman, P. (eds) (1996). *Socioeconomic Inequalities and Health. Proceedings of the Socioeconomic Inequalities and Health Conference, Wellington, 9–10 December*. Wellington: Institute of Policy Studies.

Cumming, J. and Scott, C.D. (1998). The role of outputs and outcomes in purchaser accountability, *Health Policy*, December: 53–68.

Cumming, J., Salmond, G. and Mooney, G. (1994). *Priority Setting: Choosing the Rational Road*, discussion paper no. 1. Wellington: Health Services Research Centre.

Cutler, D.M. (1994). A guide to health care reform, *The Journal of Economic Perspectives*, 8(3): 13–31.

Daniels, N., Light, D.W. and Caplan, R.L. (1996). *Benchmarks for Fairness for Health Care Reform*. Oxford: Oxford University Press.

Danzon, P.M. (1992). Hidden overhead costs: is Canada's system really less expensive?, *Health Affairs*, 11: 21–43.

Davis, K. (1999). International health policy: common problems, alternative strategies, *Health Affairs*, 18(3): 135–43.

Davis, K., Anderson, G.F., Rowland, D. and Steinberg, E.P. (1990). *Health Care Cost Containment*. Baltimore: Johns Hopkins University Press.

De Abreu Lourenco, R., Foulds, K., Smoker, I. and Hall, J. (1999). *The Australian Health Care System*, CHERE discussion paper. Sydney: Centre for Health Economics, Research and Evaluation, Department of Public Health, University of Sydney.

Deber, D. and Baranek, P. (1998). Canada: markets at the margin, in W. Ranade (ed.) *Markets and Health Care: A Comparative Analysis*. Harlow: Addison Wesley Longman.

De Leon, P. and Resnick-Terry, P. (1998). Comparative policy analysis: déjà vu all over again?, *Journal of Comparative Policy Analysis: Research and Practice*, 1(1): 9–22.

Department of National Health and Welfare (1974). *A New Perspective on the Health of Canadians* (Lalonde Report). Ottawa: Department of National Health and Welfare.

Department of National Health and Welfare (1992a). Health care access and financing in Canada. Paper presented at the Four Nations Social Policy Conference, Penn State University, 15–17 September.

Department of National Health and Welfare (1992b). *OECD Health Care Reform Project.* Ottawa: Department of National Health and Welfare.

Dewdney, J. (1984). Health services in Australia, in M.W. Raffel (ed.) *Comparative Health Systems.* Pennsylvania: Penn State University.

Dewdney, J. (1987). Australia's health system – a brief description, in M.W. Raffel and N.K. Raffel (eds) *Perspectives on Health Policy: Australia, New Zealand and United States.* New York: Wiley.

Dirnfeld, V. (1996). The benefits of privatization, *Canadian Medical Association Journal*, 155(4): 407–10.

Dodson, L. (1997). Seeking cures for an ailing health system. *Australian Financial Review*, 25 July.

Donaldson C. and Mooney, G. (1993). The new NHS in a global context: is it taking us where we want to be?, *Health Policy*, 25(1/2): 9–25.

Dow, S. (1997). Health ministers to battle costs, *Age (Melbourne)*, 2 August.

Dowd, S.B. and Tilson, E.R. (1998). Health care's future? Look to the past, *Hospital Material Management Quarterly (Rockville)*, 20(1): 1–7.

Drummond, M. (1995). Evaluating Britain's NHS reforms: we may never know, *Healthcover*, February/March: 55–9.

Dunlop, D.W. and Martins, J.M. (1995). *An International Assessment of Health Care Financing: Lessons for Developing Countries.*, EDI Seminar Series. Washington, DC: The World Bank.

Dunning, A.J. (1992). *Choices in Health Care: A Report by the Government Committee on Choices in Health Care.* Rijswijk, The Netherlands: Ministry of Welfare, Health and Culture.

Eckholm, E. (1994). While Congress remains silent, health care transforms itself, *New York Times*, 18 December.

Egger, E. (1999). Best outcome may be salvation for shrivelling managed care cost savings, *Health Care Strategic Management (Chicago)*, 17(3): 12–13.

Enthoven, A. (1993). Market reform and universal coverage: avoid market failure, *Health Care Strategic Management*, February, 11–14.

Enthoven, A.C. (2000). In pursuit of an improving National Health Service, *Health Affairs*, 19(3): 102–19.

Enthoven, A.C. and Kronick, R. (1989). A consumer choice health plan for the 1990s, *New England Journal of Medicine*, 320: 29–37, 94–101.

EOHCS (European Observatory on Health Care Systems) (1998). *Health Care Systems in Transition: Canada. www.observatory.dk/index*

EOHCS (European Observatory on Health Care Systems) (1999). *Health Care Systems in Transition: United Kingdom. www.observatory.dk/index*

EOHCS (European Observatory on Health Care Systems) (2000). *Health Care Systems in Transition: Germany. www.observatory.dk/index*

Evans, R.G. (1984). *Strained Mercy: The Economics of Canadian Health Care.* Toronto: Butterworths.

Evans, R.G. (1987). Public health insurance: the collective purchase of individual care, *Health Policy*, 7: 115–34.

Evans, R.G., Barer, M.L. and Marmor, T.R. (eds) (1994). *Why Are Some People Healthy and Others Not? The Determinants of Health Populations.* New York: Aldine De Gruyter.

Fletcher, D. (1991). GP budgets put patient care at risk says watchdog, *Daily Telegraph*, 13 May, 2.

Flood, C. (1999). *International Health Care Reform: A Legal Economic and Political Analysis.* Andover: Routledge.

Folland, S., Goodman, A.C. and Stano, M. (1997). *The Economics of Health and Health Care*, 2nd edn. Englewood Cliffs, NJ: Prentice Hall.

Fromme, H. (1994). Germans are nursed to more health cover, *Lloyd's List*, 27 December, cited in Reuters News Service.

Getzen, T.E. (1997). *Health Economics: Fundamentals and Flow of Funds.* Toronto: Wiley.

Gibbs, A., Scott, J. and Fraser, D. (1988). *Unshackling the Hospitals: Report of the Task Force on Hospitals and Related Services.* Wellington: Government Printer.

Ginzberg, E. (ed.) (1994). *Critical Issues in US Health Reform.* Boulder, CO: Westview Press.

Glaser, W.A. (1991). *Health Insurance in Practice.* San Francisco: Jossey-Bass.

Glennerster, H. and Matsaganis, M. (1994). The English and Swedish Health Reforms, *International Journal of Health Services*, 24(2): 231–51.

Go, R.A. (1994). The U.S. Health Care System in Transition, *The CPA Journal*, April, 18–21.

Gold, J.S. (1993). Swallowing some bitter medicine, *Financial World*, 162(9): 24–9.

Gold, M. (1999). The changing US health care system: challenges for responsible public policy, *The Milbank Quarterly*, 77: 3–27.

Graig, L.A. (1991). Canada's national health insurance system: U.S. nemesis or model for reform? *Health of Nations: An International Perspective on U.S. Health Care Reform.* Chicago, IL: Wyatt.

Gray, G. (1996). Reform and reaction in Australian health policy, *Journal of Health Politics and Law*, 21(3): 587–615.

Gray, J. (1994). Curing the ills of the NHS market reforms, *Public Finance*, 7 January, 10–11.

Griffith, B., Iliffe, S. and Rayner, G. (1987). *Banking on Sickness.* London: Lawrence & Wishart.

Griffiths, R. (1983). *NHS Management Inquiry.* London: Department of Health and Social Security.

Hall, J. (1999). Incremental change in the Australian health care system, *Health Affairs*, 18(3): 95–110.

Hall, J., Shiell, A. and CHERE (1993). *Health Outcomes: A Health Economics Perspective*, discussion paper no. 19. Sydney: Centre for Health Economics, Research and Evaluation, Department of Public Health, University of Sydney.

Ham, C. (1992). Doctors' power, patients' risk – NHS fund-holding, *The Guardian*, 25 March: 23.

Ham, C. (1995). Profiting from the NHS, *British Medical Journal*, 310: 415–16.

Ham, C. (1997). *Health Care Reform: Learning From International Experience*. Buckingham: Open University Press.

Ham, C. (1999). The third way in health care reform: does the emperor have any clothes?, *Journal of Health Services Research and Policy*, 4(3): 1–6.

Hancock, L. (1999). *Health Policy in the United States*. St Leonards, NSW: Allen & Unwin.

Harrop, M. (ed.) (1992). *Power and Policy in Liberal Democracies*. Cambridge: Cambridge University Press.

Haussler, B. (1993). View from Germany, *Quality in Health Care*, 2: 63–4.

Health Insurance Commission (1998). *Health Insurance*. Canberra: ACT.

Heidenheimer, A.J., Heclo, H. and Adams, C.T. (1990). *Comparative Public Policy: The Politics of Social Choice in America, Europe and Japan*. New York: St Martin's Press.

Heidenmann, E. (1994). The Canadian health care system: cost and quality, *Bulletin of PAHO*, 28(2): 169–76.

Higgins, J. (1988). *The Business of Medicine: Private Health Care in Britain*. Hong Kong: Macmillan Education.

Higgins, J. and Ruddle, S. (1991). Waiting for a better alternative, *Health Service Journal*, 11 July: 18–19.

Holland, W.W. (1994). Commentary: Recent reforms in the British National Health Service – lessons for the United States, *American Journal of Public Health*, 84(2): 186–9.

Howlett, M. and Ramesh (1995). *Studying Public Policy: Policy Cycles and Policy Subsystems*. Toronto: Oxford University Press.

Hsiao, W.C. (1992). Introduction: Comparing health care systems – what nations can learn from one another, *Journal of Health Politics, Policy and Law*, 17(4): 613–36.

Hudson, T., Haugh, R. and Serb, C. (1999). Off Target, *Hospitals and Health Networks*, 73: 34–43.

Hughes, D. and McGuire, A. (1992). Legislating for health: the changing nature of regulation in the NHS, in R. Dirgwell and P. Fenn *Quality and Regulation in Health Care*. London: Routledge.

Iannantuono, A. and Eyles, J. (1997). Meanings in policy: a textual analysis of Canada's 'Achieving Health for All' document, *Scientific Medicine*, 44(11): 1611–21.

Industry Commission (1997). *Private Health Insurance*. Canberra: Australian Government Publishing Service.

Jackson, J.L. (1996). The Dutch health care system: lessons for reform in the United States, *Southern American Journal*, 89(6): 567–72.

Jacob, J.A. (1998). HMOs will hike premiums as estimated 8.3% in 1999, *American Medical News*, 2 November: 12–16.

Jacobs, A. (1998). Seeing difference: market health reform in Europe, *Journal of Health Politics, Policy and Law*, 23(1): 1–33.

James, J.H. (1995). Reforming the British National Health Service: implementation problems in London, *Journal of Health Politics, Policy and Law*, 20(1): 191–210.

Janssen, R. and van der Made, J. (1990). Privatisation in health care: concepts, motives and policies, *Health Policy*, 14: 191–202.

Jérôme-Forget, M., White, J. and Wiener, J.M. (eds) (1995). *Health Care Reforms through Internal Markets*. Montreal: Institute for Research on Public Policy.

Johnsson, J. (1996). HMOs dominate, shape the market (health maintenance organizations – industry overview), *American Medical News*, 39(4): 1–3.

Jost, T. (1998). German health care reform: the next steps, *Journal of Health Politics, Policy and Law*, 23(4): 697–712.

Kamke, K. (1997). The German health care system and health care reform, *Health Policy*, 43: 171–94.

Kirk, D. (1993). German employers plead for health reforms, *Business Insurance*, 27: 13–16.

Kirk, D.L. (1994). Health rates to drop: German insurance losses, *Business Insurance*, 19 September, cited in Reuters News Service.

Kirkman-Liff, B. (1997). The United States, in C. Ham (ed.) *Health Care Reform: Learning from International Experience*. Buckingham: Open University Press, chapter 2.

Kirkman-Liff, B.L. and van de Ven, W.P.M.M. (1989). Improving efficiency in the Dutch health care system: current innovations and future options, *Health Policy*, 13: 35–53.

Kirkup, W. and Donaldson, L.J. (1994). Is health care a commodity: how will purchasing improve the National Health Service?, *Journal of Public Health Medicine*, 16(3): 256–62.

Klein, R. (1994). Can we restrict the health care menu? *Health Policy*, 27: 103–12.

Klein, R. (1995). Big bang health care reform – does it work? The case of Britain's 1991 National Health Service Reforms, *The Milbank Quarterly*, 73(3): 299–337.

Klein, R. (1998). Why Britain is reorganizing its National Health Service – yet again, *Health Affairs*, July/August: 111–23.

Klein, R., Day, R. and Redmayne, S. (1996). *Managing Scarcity*. Buckingham: Open University Press.

Kovach, K.A. (1998). Managed care: what's next? *Business and Economic Review (Columbia)*, 45(1): 19–22.

Lapré, R.M. (1988). A change in the direction of the Dutch health care system? *Health Policy*, 10: 21–32.

Leatt, P. and Williams, A.P. (1997). The health system of Canada, in M. Raffel (ed.) *Health Care and Reform in Industrialised Countries*. Pennsylvania: Pennsylvania State University.

172   *Public and private roles in health care systems*

Leeder, S.R. (1998). Mixed heritage, uncertain future in healthcare. (country profile: Australia), *The Lancet*, 351: 1570.

Le Grand, J. (1991). *The Distribution of Public Expenditure on Health Care Revisited.* London: London School of Economics.

Le Grand, J. (1999). Competition, cooperation or control? Tales from the British National Health Service, *Health Affairs*, 18(3): 27–39.

Le Grand, J., Mays, N. and Mulligan, J-A. (1998). *Learning from the NHS Internal Market. A Review of Evidence.* London: King's Fund Publishing.

Light, D.W. (1992). The radical experiment: transforming Britain's national health system to interlocking markets, *Journal of Public Health Policy*, 13(2): 146–79.

Loff, B. and Cordner, S. (1999). Indigenous Australian health survey, *The Lancet*, 352(i9152): 568(1).

Lovelace, C. and Sedgwick, J. (1996). Policy strategies and reform trends in Canada and New Zealand. Paper presented at the WHO (European Regional Office) Ljubljana Conference, 22 January.

Maarse, J.A.M. (1989). Hospital budgeting in Holland: aspects, trends and effects, *Health Policy*, 11: 257–76.

Macbeth, H. (ed.) (1996). *Health Outcomes: Biological, Social and Economic Perspectives.* Oxford: Oxford University Press.

Madden, T.A. (1991). The reform of the British National Health Service, *Journal of Public Health Policy*, 12(3): 378–96.

Maddock, S. and Morgan, G. (1998). Barriers to transformation: beyond bureaucracy and the market conditions for collaboration in health and social care, *International Journal of Public Sector Management*, 11(4): 234–51.

Malcolm, L. (1997). GP budgetholding in New Zealand: lessons for Britain and elsewhere, *British Medical Journal*, 314(7098): 1890–2.

Markandya, A. (ed.) (1992). *The Earthscan Reader in Environmental Economics.* London: Earthscan Publications.

Marmor, T.R. (1993). Commentary on Canadian health insurance: lessons for the United States, *International Journal of Health Sciences*, 23(1): 45–62.

Marmor, T. R. (1997). Global health policy reform: misleading mythology or learning opportunity, in C. Altensetter and J.W. Bjorkman (eds) *Health Policy Reform: National Variations and Globalization.* London: Macmillan.

Marmor, T.R. (1998). *Market Limits to Health Care Reform: Public Success, Private Failure.* London: Routledge.

Mason, A. and Morgan, K. (1995). Purchaser–provider: the international dimension, *British Medical Journal*, 310: 231–5.

Matsaganis, M. and Glennerster, H. (1994). The threat of 'cream skimming' in the post-reform NHS, *Journal of Health Economics*, 13: 31–60.

Maynard, A. (1991). Developing the health care market, *The Economic Journal*, 10: 1277–86.

Maynard, A. (1995). Health care reform: don't confuse me with facts, stupid! Four Country Conference on Health Care Reforms and Health Care Policies in the United States, Canada, Germany and the Netherlands. Amsterdam/Rotterdam, 23–5 February.

McClelland, M. (1991). Concepts of equity, in *Fair Health? Equity and the Health System*. Canberra: Australian National Health Strategy.

McDonald, J. (1998). A social experiment that keeps adapting (Australia's public health system), *British Medical Journal*, 317(4): 55.

McNaught, A. (1988). *Race and Health Policy*. London: Croom Helm.

Ministry of Health (1998). *Health Expenditure Trends in New Zealand 1980–1997*. Wellington: Ministry of Health.

Ministry of Welfare, Health and Cultural Affairs (1988). *Changing Health Care in the Netherlands*. Rijswijk: Ministry of Welfare, Health and Cultural Affairs.

Ministry of Welfare, Health and Cultural Affairs (1996). *Health Insurance in the Netherlands*. Rijswijk: Ministry of Welfare, Health and Cultural Affairs.

Minton, E. (1996). Tricare: on the front lines, *Independent Living Provider*, 11: 14–15.

Mitnick, B.M. (1980). *The Political Economy of Regulation*. New York: Columbia University Press.

Moon, M. (1994). The role of Medicare in reform, in E. Ginzberg (ed.) *Critical Issues in U.S. Health Reform*. Boulder, CO: Westview Press, pp. 171–89.

Moon, M. and Holahan, J. (1992). Can states take the lead in health care reform?, *JAMA*, 268(12): 1588–94.

Moran, M. (1992). The health-care state in Europe: convergence or divergence, *Environment and Planning*, 10: 77–90.

Morgello, C. (1993). Controlling health care costs, *Institutional Investor*, 30 September: 29–31.

Musgrove, P. (1996). *Public and Private Roles in Health: Theory and Financing Patterns*, World Bank Discovery Paper no. 339. Washington, DC: World Bank.

Naylor, D.C. (1992). The Canadian health care system: a model for America to emulate, *Health Economics*, l: 19–37.

Naylor, D.C. (1999). Canada under fiscal duress, *Health Affairs*, 18(3): 10–25.

Navarro, V. (1991). The West German health care system: a critique. *International Journal of Health Services*, 21(3): 565–71.

NERA (National Economic Research Associates) (1993). *The Health Care System, New Zealand*. Dordrecht, The Netherlands: Kluwer.

NERA (National Economic Research Associates) (1993). *The Health Care System in the United States*. Dordrecht, The Netherlands: Kluwer.

Neuschler, E. (1990). *Research Bulletin: Canadian Health Care*. New York: Health Insurance Association of America.

Oakley, P. and Greaves, E. (1995). Decentralisation, *Health Services Journal*, 9 February: 30–1.

O'Donnell, O. and Popper, C. (1989). *Equity and the Distribution of*

National Health Service Resources. London: London School of Economics.

OECD (1992). *The Reform of Health Care: A Comparative Analysis of Seven OECD Countries.* Paris: OECD.

OECD (1994). *The Reform of Health Systems.* Paris: OECD.

OECD (1997). *Health Data 1997.* Paris: OECD.

OECD (1998). *Health Data 1998. A Comparative Analysis of Twenty-nine Countries.* Paris: OECD.

OECD (1999). *Health Data 1999. A Comparative Analysis of Twenty-nine Countries.* Paris: OECD.

Okma, K.G.H. (1997). The balancing act of a health minister: controlling health expenditures in the Netherlands. LSE Health Annual Lecture, London, 5 November.

Okma, K.G.H. (1998). Editorial: Changing patients – why, when and how? *Journal of Health Services Research and Policy*, 3(3): 131–4.

Osbourne, D. and Gaebler, T. (1992). *Reinventing Government.* Reading: Addison-Wesley.

Pallot, P. (1992). NHS 'should be proud of waiting list cuts', *The Independent*, 13 May: 4.

Palmer, G.R. and Short, S.D. (1994). *Health Care and Public Policy: An Australian Analysis.* Melbourne: Macmillan Education (first published 1989).

Parkin, D. (1989). Comparing health service efficiency across countries, *Oxford Review of Economic Policy*, 5(1): 75–88.

Peabody, J.W., Bickel, S.R. and Lawson, J.S. (1996). The Australian health care system: are the incentives down under right side up?, *Journal of American Medical Association*, 276(24): 1944–50.

Peterson, M.A. (1998). *Healthy Markets? The New Competition in Medical Care.* Durham, NC: Duke University Press.

Phelps, C.E. (1997). *Health Economics*, 2nd edn. Reading: Addison Wesley Longman.

Podger, A. (1999). Reforming the Australian health care system: a government perspective, *Health Affairs*, 18(3): 111–13.

Powell, M.A. (1997). *Evaluation the National Health Service.* Buckingham: Open University Press.

Propper, C. (1995). Regulatory reform of the NHS internal market, *Health Economics*, 4: 77–83.

Radical Statistics Health Group (1995). NHS 'indicators of success': what do they tell us? *British Medical Journal*, 310: 1045–50.

Raffel, M.W. (ed.) (1997). *Health Care and Reform in Industrialized Countries.* Pennsylvania: Pennsylvania State University Press.

Raffel, M.W. and Raffel, N.K. (eds) (1987). *Perspectives on Health Policy: Australia, New Zealand and United States.* New York: Wiley.

Rafuse, J. (1996). Private-sector share of health spending hits record level, *Canadian Medical Association Journal*, 155(6): 749.

Ranade, W. (1994). *A Future for the NHS? Health Care in the 1990s.* London: Longman.

Ranade, W. (ed.) (1998). *Markets and Health Care: A Comparative Analysis*. Harlow: Addison Wesley Longman.

Rathwell, T. (1994). Health care in Canada: a system in turmoil, *Health Policy*, 24: 5–17.

Redwood, J. (1988). *In Sickness and in Health: Managing Change in the NHS*. London: Centre for Policy Studies.

Reinhardt, U. (1999). Mangled competition and managed whatever, *Health Affairs*, 18(3): 92–4.

Reisman, D. (1993). *The Political Economy of Health Care*. New York: St Martin's Press.

Rejda, G. (1984). *Social Insurance and Economic Security*. Englewood Cliffs, NJ: Prentice Hall.

Richardson, J. (1989). Ownership and regulation in the health care sector, in J.R.G. Butler and D.P. Doessel (eds) *Health Care Economics: Australian Readings*. Sydney: Australian Professional Publications, chapter 4.

Robinson, R. (1997). Managed competition: health care reform in the Netherlands, in W. Ranade (ed.) *Markets and Health Care: A Comparative Analysis*. London: Longmans.

Robinson, R. and Le Grand, J. (eds) (1994). *Evaluating the NHS Reforms*. London: King's Fund Institute.

Roemer, M. (1991a). *National Health Systems of the World. Volume 1: The Countries*. New York: Oxford University Press, pp. 129–35.

Roemer, M. I. (1991b). *National Health Systems of the World. Volume 2: The Issues*. New York: Oxford University Press.

Rogers, W., O'Rourke, T., Ware J., Jr, Brook, R. and Newhouse, J. (1991). Effects of cost sharing in health insurance on disability days, *Health Policy*, 18: 131–9.

Rosenthal, T.C. (1997). Medicaid primary care services in New York State: partial capitation vs full capitation, *JAMA*, 277(2): 94.

Rublee, D. (1992). Health care über Alles: how it works in Germany, *Healthcare Financial Management*, 46(1): 40–7.

Ruggie, M. (1996). *Realignments in the Welfare State: Health Policy in the United States, Britain, and Canada*. New York: Columbia University Press.

Salmond, G. and Mooney, G. (eds) (1994). Special issue on New Zealand health reforms, *Health Policy*, 29: 1–182.

Salter, B. (1995). The private sector and the NHS: redefining the welfare state, *Policy and Politics*, 23(1): 17–30.

Saltman, R.B. and de Roo, A.A. (1989). Hospital policy in the Netherlands: the parameters of structural stalemate, *Journal of Health Politics, Policy and Law*, 14(4): 773–95.

Saltman, R.B. and von Otter, C. (1992). *Planned Markets and Public Competition: Strategic Reform in Northern European Health Systems*. Buckingham: Open University Press.

Saltman, R.B and von Otter, C. (eds) (1995). *Implementing Planned Markets in Health Care: Balancing Social and Economic Responsibility*. Buckingham: Open University Press.

Saltman, R.B., Figueras, J. and Sakellarides, C. (eds) (1998). *Critical Challenges for Health Care Reform in Europe.* Buckingham: Open University Press.

Scheffler, R.M. (1992). Culture versus competition: the reforms of the British National Health Service, *Journal of Public Health Policy*, 13(2): 180–5.

Schieber, G.J. (1997). *Innovations in Health Care Financing Proceedings of a World Bank Conference, March 10–11.* Washington, DC: World Bank.

Schneider, M. (1991). Health care cost containment in the Federal Republic of Germany, *Health Care Financing Review*, 12(3): 87–101.

Schneider, M., Denerlein, R.K-H., Köse, A. and Scholles, L. (1992). The Netherlands, *Health Policy*, 20(1/2): 73–82, 199–209.

Schoen, C. and Zacharias, L. (1994). Federal and state public employees health benefits programs, in E. Ginzberg (ed.) *Critical Issues in U.S. Health Reform.* Boulder, CO: Westview Press, pp. 208–47.

Schofield, D. (1997). *Private Health Insurance and Community Rating: Who Has Benefited?* Canberra: AIHW.

Schulenburg, J. and von der Graf, M. (1994). Forming and reforming the market for third-party purchasing of health care: a German perspective, *Social Science and Medicine*, 39(10): 1473–81.

Schut, F.T. and van de Ven, W.P.M.M. (eds) (1987). *Proceedings of the Conference on Regulated Competition in the Dutch Health Care System.* Rotterdam: Department of Health Policy and Management, Erasmus University.

Schut, F.T., Greenburg, W. and van de Ven, W.P.M.M. (1991). Antitrust policy in the Dutch health care system and the relevance of EEC competition policy and US antitrust practice, *Health Policy*, 17: 257–84.

Schwartz, F. and Busse, R. (1997). Germany, in C. Ham (ed.) *Health Care Reform: Learning from International Experience.* Buckingham: Open University Press, chapter 6.

Scott, C.D. (1994). Reform of the New Zealand health care system, *Health Policy*, 25: 25–40.

Scott, C., Fougere, G. and Marwick, J. (1986). *Choices for Health Care*, Wellington: Government Printer.

Scott, G., McKenzie, L. and Webster, J. (2000). New Zealand case study, in A.S. Preker and A. Harding (eds) *Innovations in Health Service Delivery, Vol. 1: The Corporatization of Public Hospitals.* Baltimore, MD: Johns Hopkins University Press.

Secretary of State for Health (1997). *The New NHS – Modern, Dependable*, CM 3807. London: HMSO.

Shackley, P. and Healey, A. (1993). Creating a market: an economic analysis of the purchaser–provider model, *Health Policy*, 25(1): 153–68.

Shalala, D.E. and Reinhardt, U.E. (1999). Interviewing the U.S. health care system from within: candid talk from HHS, *Health Affairs,* 18(3): 46–55.

Sheils, J.F., Young, G.R. and Rubin, R.J. (1992). O Canada: do we expect too much from its health system? *Health Affairs*, 11(1): 7–20.

Sheldon, T.A. (1993). Changing the measure of quality in the NHS: from purchasing activity to purchasing protocols, *Quality in Health Care*, 2: 149–50.

Sloan, J. (1997). Tinkering overlooks the core problems, *Australian*, 11 April.

Spanjer, M. (1996). New Dutch insurance contributions planned, *The Lancet*, 348: 885.

Stoddart, G.L. and Barer, M.L. (1992). Toward integrated medical resource policies for Canada. 6: Remuneration of physicians and global expenditure policy, *Canadian Medical Association Journal*, 147(1): 33–8.

Stone, D. (1991). German unification: east meets west in the doctor's office, *Journal of Health Politics, Policy and Law*, 16(2): 401–12.

Termeer, H.A. and Raines, L.J. (1994). Finding a lasting cure for U.S. health care, *Harvard Business Review*, 72 (Sept./Oct.): 45–63.

Thorne, J.L., Bianchi, B., Bonnyman, G. and Leddy, T. (1995). State perspectives on health care reform: Oregon, Hawaii, Tennessee, and Rhode Island (Medicaid and State Health Reform), *Health Care Financing Review*, 16(3): 121–39.

Thust, W. (1988). Political–medical allocations in the compulsory health insurance program in the Federal Republic of Germany, in H. Sass and R. Massey (eds) *Health Care Systems: Moral Conflicts in European and American Public Policy*. Dordrecht: Kluwer, pp. 255–65.

Tiesberg, E.O., Porter, M.E. and Brown, G.B. (1994). Making competition in health care work, *Harvard Business Review*, 72 (July/Aug.): 131–41.

Tuohy, C.H. (1999). Dynamics of a changing health sphere: the United States, Britain, and Canada, *Health Affairs*, 18(3): 114–33.

Upton, S. (1991). *Your Health and the Public Health*. Wellington: GP Print Limited.

van de Ven, W.P.M.M. (1990a). From regulated cartel to regulated competition in the Dutch health care system, *European Economic Review*, 34: 632–45.

van de Ven, W.P.M.M. (1990b). *Perestrojka in the Dutch Health Care System: A Demonstration Project for Other European Countries*. Rotterdam: Department of Health Policy and Management, Erasmus University.

van de Ven, W.P.M.M. (1997). The Netherlands, in C. Ham (ed.) *Health Care Reform: Learning from International Experience*. Buckingham: Open University Press.

van der Grinten, T.E.D. (1996). Conditions for health care reform: changing the policy system of Dutch health care, *Four Country Conference: Health Care Reform, Conference Report, Chateau Montebello, Canada, 16–18 May*.

van Doorslaer, E., Wagstaff, A. and Rutten, F. (1993). *Equity in the Finance and Delivery of Health Care: An International Perspective*. Oxford: Oxford University Press.

Wall, A. (1996). *Health Care Systems in Liberal Democracies*. London: Routledge.

Walt, G. (1998). *Health Policy: An Introduction to Process and Power*. London: Zed Books.

Warner, M. (1997). *Redesigning Health Services: Reducing the Zone of Delusion*. London: Nuffield Trust.

Weale, A. (ed.) (1988). *Cost and Choice in Health Care: The Ethical Dimension*. London: King Edward's Hospital Fund for London.

Weil, T.P. (1992). The German health care system: a model for hospital reform in the United States?, *Hospital and Health Services Administration*, 37(4): 533–8.

Weil, T.P. (1996). How health networks and HMOs could result in public utility regulation health maintenance organisations, *Hospital and Health Service Administration*, 41(2): 266–82.

Weimer, D.L. and Vining, A.R. (1999). *Policy Analysis: Concepts and Practice*. Englewood Cliffs, NJ: Prentice Hall.

Weiner, J.M. (1994). Managed Competition as Financing Reform: A View from the United States. Paper presented at the Institute for Research on Public Policy/ Brookings Institution international conference, 'Health Care Cost Control: Internal Market Mechanisms', Montreal, Canada, 15–16 May.

Weiner, J.M. and de Lissovoy, G. (1993). Razing a Tower of Babel: a taxonomy for managed care and health insurance, *Journal of Health Politics, Policy and Law*, 16(1): 75–113.

Weiner, S, Maxwell, J., Sapolsky, H., Dunn, D. and Hsiao, W. (1987). Economic incentives and organizational realities: managing hospitals under DRGs, *The Milbank Quarterly*, 65(4): 463–87.

Weisbrod, B.A. (1991). The health care quadrilemma: an essay on technical change, insurance, quality of care, and cost containment, *Journal of Economic Literature*, 29 (June): 523–52.

West, P.A. (1988). *Understanding the NHS: A Question of Incentives*. London: King Edward's Hospital Fund for London.

Wheelwright, K. (1995). Commonwealth and state powers in health – a constitutional diagnosis, *Monash University Law Review*, 21(1): 53–83.

White, J. (1995). *Competing Solutions: American Health Care Proposals and International Experience*. Washington, DC: Brookings Institution.

Whitehead, M. (1994). Is it fair? Evaluating the equity implications of the NHS reforms, in R. Robinson and J. Le Grand (eds) *Evaluating the NHS Reforms*. London: King's Fund Institute, pp. 208–42.

Wysong, J. and Abel, T. (1990). Universal health insurance and high-risk groups in West Germany: implications for U.S. health policy, *The Milbank Quarterly*, 68(4): 527–60.

York, G. (1992). Fee-for-service: cashing in on the Canadian medical care system, *Journal of Public Health Policy*, 13(2): 140–5.

Zweifel, P. and Frech, H.E., III (1992). *Health Economics Worldwide*. Dordrecht: Kluwer.

INDEX

THE GLOBAL CHALLENGE OF HEALTH CARE RATIONING

Angela Coulter and Chris Ham (eds)

Rationing or priority setting occurs in all health care systems. Doctors, managers, and politicians are involved in making decisions on how to use scarce resources and which groups and patients should receive priority. These decisions may be informed by the results of medical research and cost effectiveness studies but they also involve the use of judgement and experience. Consequently, priority setting involves ethics as well as economics and decisions on who should live and who should die remain controversial and contested.

This book seeks to illuminate the debate on priority setting by drawing on experience from around the world. The authors are all involved in priority setting, either as decision-makers or researchers, and their contributions demonstrate in practical terms how different countries and disciplines are approaching the allocation of resources between competing claims. Accessible to general readers as well as specialists, *The Global Challenge of Health Care Rationing* summarizes the latest thinking in this area and provides a unique resource for those searching for a guide through the maze.

Contents
Introduction – Part 1: How to set priorities – Part 2: Governments and rationing – Part 3: Priorities in developing countries – Part 4: Ethical dilemmas – Part 5: Techniques for determining priorities – Part 6: Involving the public – Part 7: rationing specific treatments – Conclusion – References – Index.

288 pp   0 335 20463 5 (Paperback)   0 335 20464 3 (Hardback)

CRITICAL CHALLENGES FOR HEALTH CARE REFORM IN EUROPE

Richard B. Saltman, Josep Figueras and Constantino Sakellarides

This volume explores the central issues driving the present process of health care reform in Europe. More than 30 scholars and policy-makers from all parts of Europe draw together the available evidence from epidemiology and public health, economics, public policy, organizational behaviour and management theory as well as real world policy-making experience, to lay out the options that health sector decision-makers confront. Through its cross-disciplinary, cross-national approach, the book highlights the underlying trends that now influence health policy formulation across Europe. An authoritative introduction provides a broad synthesis of present trends and strategies in European health policy.

Contents

Introduction – Part I: The context for health reform – Part II: Demand-side strategies – Part III: Supply side strategies – Part IV: On state, citizen and society – Part V: Implementing health reform – Assessing the evidence – Index.

448 pp   0 335 19970 4 (Paperback)   0 335 19971 2 (hardback)